Routledge Revivals

Public Investment Criteria

This book, first published in 1967, explores some of the problems formulating investment criteria for the public sector of a mixed-enterprise, underdeveloped economy. The typical essay on public investment criteria explicitly or implicitly postulates a single goal for economic analysis – maximization of weighted average of national income over time – and relegates all other objectives of public policy to a limbo of "political" and "social" objectives not amenable to systematic, rational treatment. In contrast Professor Marglin assumes a multiplicity of objectives and explores ways and means of expressing contributions to different objectives in common terms. The book also investigates the relationship of specific investment criteria to the objectives of public policy. Benefits and costs are defined separately for each objective, as are so-called "secondary" benefits. This book is suited for students of economics.

Public Investment Criteria

Benefit Cost-Analysis for Planned Economic Growth

Stephen A. Marglin

ROUTLEDGE REVIVALS

Routledge
Taylor & Francis Group

First published in 1967
by George Allen & Unwin Ltd

This edition first published in 2015 by Routledge
2 Park Square, Milton Park, Abingdon, Oxon, OX14 4RN
and by Routledge
711 Third Avenue, New York, NY 10017

Routledge is an imprint of the Taylor & Francis Group, an informa business

Publisher's Note
The publisher has gone to great lengths to ensure the quality of this reprint but points out that some imperfections in the original copies may be apparent.

Disclaimer
The publisher has made every effort to trace copyright holders and welcomes correspondence from those they have been unable to contact.

A Library of Congress record exists under LC control number: 66022644

ISBN 13: 978-1-138-83065-3 (hbk)
ISBN 13: 978-1-315-73712-6 (ebk)

PUBLIC INVESTMENT CRITERIA

BENEFIT-COST ANALYSIS
FOR PLANNED ECONOMIC GROWTH

BY

STEPHEN A. MARGLIN

London

GEORGE ALLEN & UNWIN LTD

RUSKIN HOUSE · MUSEUM STREET

FIRST PUBLISHED IN 1967
SECOND IMPRESSION 1969

SBN: 04 332018 X CASED EDITION
SBN: 04 332041 4 PAPER EDITION

PRINTED IN GREAT BRITAIN BY
COMPTON PRINTING LIMITED
LONDON AND AYLESBURY

DEDICATION

For my friends in Dhabi Kalan,
beneficiaries of the Indian
Government's investment criteria

CONTENTS

LIST OF FIGURES

PREFACE

During a discussion in the Indian Planning Commission in the fall of 1963 I made a comment about the place of benefit-cost analysis in Indian planning and was asked to clarify my remark in a short memorandum. The memo quickly took on a logic of its own and four pages grew into the present book. The result is not wholly satisfactory, too technical to serve the purposes of the neophyte, yet containing too little that is new to make it of interest to the theorist. It might nevertheless be of some value as an introduction to the special branch of economics that concerns itself with systematic analysis of investment alternatives from the point of view of a government. The book naturally reflects Indian experiences and problems. Yet the principles it elaborates are applicable to other economies in which public enterprise plays a substantial role in development plans.

I am grateful to many individuals for their help in preparation of this book, and the list below is by no means exhaustive. Jagdish Bhagwati, Christopher Foster, Maynard Hufschmidt, Arthur Maass, Alan Manne, and Amartya Sen all read the first draft, and their suggestions—only a small number of which could be conveniently acknowledged—are reflected throughout the present version. Thomas Weisskopf was extremely helpful in correcting misapprehensions about the treatment of foreign exchange; unfortunately his counsel came too late to be fully reflected in the pages that follow. Jean Clark's careful editing sharpened the presentation. V. S. Mani provided invaluable assistance in many ways over a period of two years. To him and his colleagues who kept office and home running so smoothly that I felt more like a prince than a professor, I owe a debt of gratitude which I shall never be able to repay adequately.

STEPHEN A. MARGLIN

Cambridge, Massachusetts
January 1966

CHAPTER 1

SUPERSTRUCTURE

Introduction: A Capsule History of Benefit-Cost Analysis

This essay explores some of the theoretical problems of subjecting public investment decisions to quantitative economic analysis, commonly called benefit-cost analysis. Benefit-cost analysis applies to decisions at the tactical level—the product-mix, size, location, capital intensity, durability, and other aspects of the design of individual projects, enterprises, and programmes of closely related projects and enterprises that the strategy of development has assigned to the public sector. There is no discussion here of which activities the government of a developing economy ought to undertake, nor is there discussion of how the over-all plan targets for various branches of public investment ought to be reached, omissions that would be inexcusable if this book pretended to present a complete strategy of public expenditure. But it does not. Benefit-cost analysis is an aid to implementation of the strategy of development, not a substitute for strategy.

The goal of benefit-cost analysis and of economic choice in general can be stated as maximization of utility subject to whatever constraints the economic and political environment imposes. "Utility" is relatively easy to specify in some cases. A private firm is one example: For many purposes we do not go far wrong if we hypothesize that a firm's utility is its monetary profit and that a firm therefore seeks to maximize the difference between its monetary revenues and monetary costs. The utility function is much more difficult to specify in other cases. In particular, there is no simple way to describe the desirable and deleterious effects of economic activity from the point of view of a government, and one of the major conceptual problems of subjecting public investment decisions to economic analysis lies in defining the government's utility function. Only when this has been done is it possible to make our notions of benefits and costs sufficiently meaningful that quantitative appraisal of economic alternatives within the public sector can be expected to lead to a higher level of performance than more intuitive methods of decision-making permit.

The credit for the seminal intellectual work in benefit-cost analysis must go to the nineteenth-century Frenchman Jules Dupuit [7], who seems to have been the first to explore systematically the distinctive features of the utility function of a government. He recognized, among other things, the existence of "consumers' surplus"[1] and proposed that the benefits to the community of public enterprises like bridges and roads are not the revenues generated to the public treasury, the actual payments of the public, but the public's willingness to pay, that is, the sum of actual payments and consumers' surplus.

The first systematic attempt to apply benefit-cost analysis to public economic decisions seems, however, to have taken place on the other side of the Atlantic—as a result of the expansion of public investment activity in the United States, especially in water-resources development, during the 1930's. A key document in the development of benefit-cost analysis in America was the Flood Control Act of 1936,[2] which set forth as a standard in the evaluation of proposals for water-resources development the requirement that "the benefits to whomsoever they may accrue [be] in excess of the estimated costs." Subsequently, economic analysis—benefit-cost analysis—designed to demonstrate that this standard was being met accompanied the technical analysis of proposed investment projects.

However, the 1936 act did not spell out the criteria by which benefits and costs were to be measured, and the several public agencies with (overlapping) responsibilities in the area of water-resources development[3] took this task upon themselves. It is

[1] "Consumers' surplus" is the difference between the maximum amount consumers are willing to pay for a specified quantity of a good rather than go without it and the value of the given quantity at the good's competitive market price.

[2] 49 Stat. 1570.

[3] Some of these agencies are the Army Corps of Engineers, whose responsibilities date from an era in which America's rivers were essential lines of communication for her defence; the Bureau of Reclamation, a division of the Department of the Interior, with responsibilities for river development in seventeen arid and semiarid Western states; the Soil Conservation Service (Department of Agriculture), with responsibilities

only natural that each agency developed evaluation criteria favourable to its own programme and that disagreement arose about the criteria. In 1950 an interagency committee attempted to introduce uniformity into the standards and criteria employed in plan formulation and evaluation, but the practices proposed in this committee's *Green Book* [28] have never attained official standing. The Bureau of the Budget, which enters the picture because it reviews all proposals for project authorizations as well as for appropriations before their transmission from the White House to Congress, subsequently developed a set of criteria by which *it* would henceforth evaluate all proposals received from the line agencies. *Budget Circular A-47* [27] was issued in 1952, and, despite opposition from line agencies and their congressional allies on the grounds that it took an overly narrow "accountant's" view of the contributions of river development projects to the nation, this memorandum remained the basis for appraisal by the Budget Bureau throughout the Eisenhower Administration.

President Kennedy's February 1961 message to Congress on natural resources promised a review of standards and criteria for river development, and to implement this promise a panel of consultants was asked by the director of the Bureau of the Budget to assess the existing criteria and propose changes. The report of this panel, called the *Consultants' Report* [29], was completed in June 1961. However, attacks on the Budget Bureau because of the restrictive nature of its earlier standards put the Bureau so much on the defensive that it felt it wise to disavow claims to leadership in the formulation of investment criteria and to disavow this report *pari passu.* A new interagency committee was subsequently appointed to investigate water-resources investment criteria, and its recommendations, published as Senate Document No. 97, 87th Congress [30], were approved by President Kennedy in May 1962 for application by the line agencies and the Budget Bureau.

This capsule history is intended not only to serve as an introduction to US Government literature on benefit-cost

in the development of small watersheds; and the Tennessee Valley Authority, an autonomous government agency that constructed and now manages the multiple-purpose development on the Tennessee River and its tributaries.

analysis but also to bring out two points relevant to the role of benefit-cost analysis in Indian planning. First, benefit-cost analysis evolved in the context of an unplanned economy radically different from India's. The United States has no framework for planned growth to achieve stated social objectives from which specific criteria might be drawn, and disagreement about the objectives of public investment has been at the heart of much of the controversy about specific criteria among line agencies, between the agencies and the Budget Bureau, and between the Budget Bureau and Congress. Second, benefit-cost analysis was introduced as a means of project "justification" alone (this word is used in the US Government literature), not as a tool for project planning; in American practice (as distinct from theory) it often has served as window dressing for projects whose plans have already been formulated with little if any reference to economic criteria.[1]

Benefit-Cost Analysis in a Planned Economy

Benefit-cost analysis in Indian planning ought to differ from its American cousin on both counts. Investment criteria for the public sector (like licensing criteria for the private sector) should be explicitly related to the objectives of growth, and these criteria should come into play in the drawing up of project plans. Perspective and five-year plans determine the broad strategy of growth by allocating resources among sectors. But the strategy of growth embodied in the plans leaves many tactical questions unresolved, and it is these tactical decisions that are the province of benefit-cost analysis.

For benefit-cost analysis to fulfil this role, planning must proceed through successive stages of setting objectives, allocating resources among sectors, and deriving the criteria for designing individual projects. The essential point is the sensitivity of the specific criteria to the plans and ultimately to the mix of objectives underlying the plan: Modify the relative emphasis on different objectives and you must change both the strategy of the plan and the tactical criteria for project selection.

[1] It is true that the *Green Book* and, more especially, the *Consultants' Report* sought to have the criteria applied at the design stage, but the plea has been largely unheeded.

This schema does not rule out feedback from project selection to perspective and quinquennial plans and finally to the objectives themselves. Since the relative emphasis among the objectives, the plans, and the investment criteria must initially be set in the absence of technological information that becomes available only as the criteria are implemented, the process of implementation might suggest revisions all the way up the planning ladder.

I would claim three virtues for this planning schema as against what I gather to be the current practice of bringing objectives to bear on project planning on a largely *ad hoc* basis. First, it would aid materially in reducing differences in the marginal effectiveness of alternative measures for accomplishing objectives (for example, between irrigation and other means of raising agricultural production). Second, it would make it possible to spell out the costs of fulfilling one objective in terms of gains sacrificed with respect to others. Finally, although no institutional framework can guarantee that the national interest will hold sway against special interests in project planning, it would be harder for any particular group to distort project plans to serve its own interests if its consent, along with the consent of other relevant sections of the community, were obtained at the time of setting the criteria—*in advance of planning specific projects*. Before specific projects are at issue, the difference in outcomes of different sets of criteria are not known, and contributions to political debate can focus upon the propriety of the criteria rather than upon the effect of the criteria on one's own economic position. Special pleading later on would then show up clearly as an attempt to gain exception from general policies already agreed upon.[1]

Objectives

The objectives most relevant to investment planning in the public sector would seem to be these four:

1. *To increase aggregate consumption.* Some would replace aggregate consumption by per capita consumption, but since population policy—as an element of development strategy

[1] See A. Maass and others [*16*], Chapter 15.

rather than tactics—is beyond the scope of this discussion, increasing aggregate and per capita consumption are identical goals.

2. *To redistribute consumption*, especially the increments provided by growth, to lower-income groups and regions in order to achieve greater equality.

The relevance of this objective to the formulation of public investment plans might be questioned. Why not design public sector projects to maximize the size of the economic pie and rely upon pricing and fiscal policies to achieve the desired slicing? The most obvious reasons are the political factors that limit the flexibility of pricing and fiscal policies. For example, consider the alternatives that often face the designers of irrigation systems, namely, whether to provide water in a relatively small geographical area for a large fraction of the acreage of each farm or to spread the same amount of water more thinly over a larger number of holdings. The second alternative in general provides a smaller net contribution to aggregate consumption, for it increases the size of the water-distribution network and the distribution costs as well as the water losses due to evaporation and absorption in the canals. In addition, the cost of supporting services like extension, credit, and the distribution of inputs complementary to water are greater because more farmers and a larger geographical area are involved. Hence if pricing and fiscal policies were perfectly flexible, the intensive alternative would be the obvious choice; any advantages of the extensive alternative on the ground that it provides a more desirable distribution of the income gains from irrigation could be realized from the intensive alternative by increasing the water tax (or price) and giving cash subsidies to the farmers deprived of irrigation. All would presumably be better off: If the pretax pie is larger with the intensive irrigation system, it can be resliced in such a way as to give everybody a larger share than that afforded by the smaller pie associated with the extensive system. The problem is that the political difficulties of increasing water-tax rates reduce the government's flexibility to redistribute income in the manner suggested, and the difficulties of cash subsidies remove whatever remaining degree of freedom there might be—note the lengths to which US policymakers have gone to disguise farm subsidies.

The only operational way to distribute the gains of irrigation widely, it would seem, is to construct extensive systems and suffer the losses in aggregate consumption this tactic entails.

Political factors may be the most important reason for eschewing reliance on pricing and fiscal policies in the pursuit of distributional goals, but there are economic grounds as well. Take pricing. Even viewed solely against the criterion of maximization of aggregate consumption, any departure from marginal-cost pricing opens the door to misallocations of resources. As for fiscal policy, all taxes and subsidies (other than lump-sum transfers, which are practicable only in a revolutionary context) distort incentives and thereby reduce aggregate consumption. Thus implementing redistributional objectives by either means—through price and fiscal policies or through incorporating redistributional objectives into public investment criteria—may lead to losses in aggregate consumption; it is a matter of judgment whether the conflict between maximizing the size of the economic pie and achieving an optimal slicing is decreased more by the one or the other means of achieving redistributional goals. In the absence of a specific preference for either tool at the level of a social objective, doubtless the course of wisdom is to rely on both direct and indirect tools.[1]

3. *To fulfil "merit wants."* Both aggregate consumption and redistribution objectives presuppose "consumer sovereignty," that is, that individuals' market valuations of alternative consumption bundles are the appropriate basis of comparison. However, for a variety of reasons policymakers may reject the preferences that individuals express in the market place in favour of politically determined consumption patterns; Richard Musgrave has labelled the goods and services thus favoured

[1] To recognize the propriety of incorporating concern for income distribution into the formulation of project plans is not to applaud every redistribution accompanying public investment programmes. Kenneth Boulding's poetic injunction apropos of the California Water Plan bears repeating:

It would be well to be quite sure
Just who *are* the deserving poor,
Or else the state-supported ditch
May serve the Undeserving Rich.

"merit wants."[1] For example, the government may decide to invest in education more heavily than market tests would suggest; or it may decide, in the interest of nutrition, to promote the production and consumption of gram and other pulses in preference to prestige cereals like wheat and rice that individuals would prefer at laissez-faire market prices.

Much has been written about the ethics of fulfilling merit wants rather than consumers' market-exhibited preferences.[2] I do not propose to enter the debate here other than to say that on Mondays, Wednesdays, and Fridays I am thoroughly convinced of the propriety of the merit-want objective, but on Tuesdays, Thursdays, and Saturdays I am equally sure that the essence of human freedom is individual choice, although the choice of ignorance for one's children or an inadequate diet seems to stretch unreasonably the range of decisions to which individual choice should apply.[3] Whatever the merits of merit wants, one has a right to be suspicious of each and every claim for preferential treatment for any particular good or service on this ground. Many so-called merit wants are in fact instances of a group redistribution objective and should be considered as such. As for the remainder, the merit-want rubric is all too tempting and convenient for anyone whose pet projects fail to pass muster on the basis of more general, individual preference-oriented objectives.

4. *To promote national self-sufficiency.* In the Indian context "self-sufficiency" has at least two interpretations: equality

[1] Merit wants should not be confused with "public" goods and services (like national defence) having the property that more for one individual cannot be at the expense of another person. (Contrast a "private" good like wheat.) Public goods by their nature cannot be supplied very well through the market, but a government can in principle allocate resources to the production of public goods in conformance with consumer sovereignty as reflected in individuals' willingness to pay. For further discussion of public goods, see Paul Samuelson [*24*], [*25*], and [*26*]; Richard Musgrave [*22*], pp. 42–89; Arthur Maass and others [*16*], pp. 44–47. On merit wants, see Musgrave [*22*], pp. 13–14.

[2] See Musgrave [*22*]; Maurice Dobb [*5*] and [*6*]; *Consultants' Report* [*29*]; and Stephen Marglin [*20*].

[3] My Tuesday–Thursday–Saturday view should not be confused with opposition to educational campaigns on the part of the government to promote merit wants, but I admit that the line between education and interference with individual choice is difficult to draw.

between the value of exports and the value of imports, including capital imports on business-like terms, or, in other words, independence from foreign aid; and the goal of autarky in order to escape the vicissitudes of foreign trade. The first meeting will be emphasized in this book.

This list of objectives may be incomplete, but many frequently listed "objectives" that have been omitted are in fact instruments for achieving those set forth above. Take, for instance, the objective of increasing employment, which all of us presumably favour in the Indian context. Insofar as this objective is not a means of increasing aggregate consumption, I believe that it is chiefly a means of redistributing consumption. Moreover, I think it is useful in clarifying the implications of alternative plans to separate these two primary components of the employment objective. Only to the extent that idleness (or leisure, to use a less pejorative term) is considered an evil in itself is increased employment really a separate objective.[1]

To list objectives, however, is not to "set" them in the sense required for derivation of operational criteria for benefit-cost analysis of projects. The relative importance of the various objectives must be specified, and, to be reflected in planning, the specification must be quantitative.

One method of specifying the relative importance of objectives lies in explicitly weighting the contribution of projects to each and formulating project plans to maximize this weighted sum of benefits. For example, consider the problem of harmonizing the objective of increasing aggregate consumption with the objective of redistributing consumption gains to the low-income region of Transylvanistan. Suppose policymakers decide that the value to the nation of a rupee generated to Transylvanistan is one and one-half times the value of a rupee generated outside of Transylvanistan. Policymakers in other words place a premium of 0·5 on consumption gains within

[1] A further objective, "moving in the direction of socialism," is an avowed goal of Indian policy. But the goal of a socialist pattern of society enters at the level of the division of economic activity between the public and private sectors rather than at the level of criteria for planning projects within the public sector. Therefore we need not concern ourselves with this objective in the present discussion.

Transylvanistan.[1] In this case the goal of project plan formulation in the public sector is to maximize the sum of gains in aggregate consumption (including Transylvan consumption) and one half the gains in consumption within Transylvanistan. Symbolically the planning goal may be written

$$\text{Max}\,\{(\text{net aggregate consumption gains}) + 0{\cdot}5\,(\text{net Transylvan consumption gains})\}. \qquad (1.1)$$

Note that there are two kinds of net benefits in this *objective function*. The multiplicity of goals renders a comparison of total benefits without the imposition of relative weights on different categories of benefits as meaningless as the addition of mangoes and bananas without the imposition of prices.

A hasty glance at objective function (1.1) might lead one to infer that far from placing special emphasis on Transylvanistan, planners are discriminating against this mythical region. For is the weight on Transylvan consumption not *less* than the weight on aggregate consumption? What this inference neglects is that in (1.1) those components of Transylvan consumption which also contribute to aggregate consumption are counted twice, once under each heading. For this reason the weight on Transylvan consumption in (1.1) has been called a premium; a weight on Transylvan consumption of 0·5 relative to aggregate consumption corresponds to a weight on Transylvan consumption of 1·5 relative to non-Transylvan consumption.

However, policymakers may be unable to decide on the basis of available knowledge whether the premium appropriate to Transylvanistan relative to the nation as a whole ought to be 0·5, 1·0, or some other number, for the value of the premium may vary with the contributions of public investment to aggregate and regional consumption. Accordingly they may prefer to resolve the conflict between the regional and national objectives by specifying a constraint on the performance of public sector programmes taken together in terms of one objective. The constraint is further subdivided among individual programmes, and the goal of all plan formulation becomes

[1] Do not object too quickly that policymakers cannot make interpersonal comparisons of this kind. They make them all the time—for example, in setting income tax rates.

maximization of the contribution of projects to the other (unconstrained) objective consistent with meeting the constraint. For example, the goal may be to choose the public investment programme that maximizes aggregate consumption gains subject to the constraint that the programme provide an increase of at least Rs 10 crores[1] in Transylvan consumption. More concisely,

Max (net aggregate consumption gains)
subject to the constraint
net Transylvan consumption gains $\geqslant$ Rs 10 crores. (1.2)

Alternatively the goal might be stated as maximization of the gains in Transylvan consumption subject to the restriction that "the benefits to whomsoever they accrue [be] in excess of the costs" by Rs 6 crores, that is, subject to the constraint that public sector programmes increase aggregate consumption by Rs 6 crores. Symbolically this goal is

Max (net Transylvan consumption gains)
subject to the constraint
net aggregate consumption gains $\geqslant$ Rs 6 crores. (1.3)

These three methods of harmonizing conflicting objectives are not as dissimilar as they may seem at first glance. Moreover, the fundamental unity underlying them has important planning consequences. Specification of constraint levels, superficially a different kind of decision from choice of a weight, *implicitly* specifies the marginal weight attaching to regional consumption relative to total consumption. A small reduction in the level of the regional income constraint in approach (1.2) would allow a small increase in aggregate consumption through marginal adjustments in the public investment programme. The ratio of the change in aggregate consumption to the change in Transylvan consumption represents an implicit marginal weight on regional consumption relative to aggregate consumption, under the assumption that the level of constraint in (1.2) accurately reflects the nation's concern for Transylvanistan relative to its concern for aggregate consumption gains.

However, at the outset of planning a public investment programme, constraint levels cannot always be established with

[1] 1 crore = 10 million.

more confidence than regional weights. If redistribution should appear inexpensive in terms of aggregate consumption losses on the basis of preliminary plans, it might be desirable to increase the gains to Transylvanistan. At the appearance of the signal of a low implicit weight for regional consumption, policymakers might be tempted to raise the minimum acceptable level of Transylvan income gains from Rs 10 crores to Rs 12 crores. On the other hand, if redistribution were extremely expensive in terms of aggregate consumption, policymakers might reduce the level of the regional gains constraint to Rs 8 crores. Analogous statements hold with respect to the other approaches to implementation of multiple objectives. A constraint on aggregate consumption might be revised in accordance with the marginal trade-off between regional and aggregate consumption, or the weight on regional consumption employed in approach (1.1) might be revised in the light of the willingness of the policymakers to trade gains with respect to one objective for gains with respect to the other. In every case revision should be made in the light of the levels of aggregate and regional consumption determined in preliminary plans.[1]

The preceding discussion can be illustrated with the help of a few diagrams. Suppose net contributions to aggregate and Transylvan consumption are measured on the axes of Figure 1.1.

The isoquant labelled W_1 represents contributions to the two objectives that policymakers deem on balance to be equally desirable. Provision from public investment programmes of the combination of Rs 10 crores of aggregate consumption and zero consumption to Transylvanistan, for example, is considered just as desirable as zero aggregate consumption and Rs 15 crores to Transylvanistan, for both combinations lie on the curve W_1. Similarly the curves W_2 and W_3 each represent equally desirable combinations of contributions; the over-all level of desirability

[1] Hollis Chenery's approach [*4*] to the implementation of multiple objectives is similar to mine, although he focuses on only two objectives (aggregate consumption and self-sufficiency) of the four analysed in this essay. Chenery provides examples drawn from the Greek experience to illustrate the impact of the self-sufficiency objective on the choice of investments. Jagdish Bhagwati's review article [*3*] on the theory of international trade discusses empirical as well as theoretical attempts to come to grips with the conflict between self-sufficiency and aggregate consumption objectives in the formulation of trade policy.

increases as we move in the direction of the arrow. The slopes of the *W*-curves represent the marginal weight, or premium, on Transylvan consumption relative to aggregate consumption. As Figure 1.1 is drawn, the value of this weight depends on the levels of aggregate and Transylvan consumption.

The curve *T* (the transformation function) represents the boundary of the set of feasible contributions to consumption for the nation as a whole and for Transylvanistan in particular. Each point on the curve represents a different public sector

NOTE: *Isoquants of a welfare function (W) show equally desirable combinations of aggregate and Transylvan consumption. The transformation function (T) shows the boundary of the set of feasible combinations. The slope of the line labelled S gives both the marginal trade-off between aggregate and Transylvan consumption and the marginal weight on Transylvan consumption (relative to aggregate consumption) that are associated with the optimal programme t.*

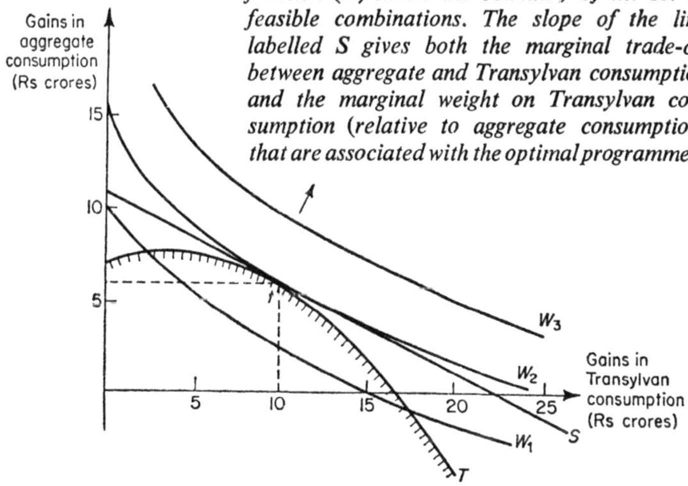

Figure 1.1. Choice of an investment programme with two objectives

investment programme; differences may be of design, of operation, or of both design and operation. As drawn, the *T*-curve tells us that the programme optimal from the point of view of aggregate consumption alone provides Rs 3 crores to Transylvanistan. Hence even if no special importance is attached to this region, that is, if the redistribution weight is zero, Rs 3 crores are contributed to Transylvan consumption. Similarly if the constraint on Transylvan consumption were set at Rs 3 crores or less, the constraint would be fulfilled without compromising the aggregate consumption objective; that is, the regional constraint would not be binding, and the perfect complementarity of objectives would emerge from the optimization process in the form of a zero marginal implicit weight on Transylvanistan relative to the nation as a whole.

The optimal programme is the one corresponding graphically to the point *t* of the *T*-curve that touches the highest *W*-isoquant attainable. This programme generates Rs 6 crores of aggregate consumption and Rs 10 crores of consumption for Transylvanistan. The slope of the separating line *S*, tangent to both W_2 and *T*, is equal both to the negative of the marginal weight on Transylvanistan relative to the nation as a whole (the slope of W_2) and to the negative of the marginal trade-off between aggregate and Transylvan consumption (the slope of *T*). As Figure 1.1 shows, a criterion for optimal investment decisions is the equality of the marginal weight and trade-off.

The equivalence of the three approaches to planning outlined earlier is illustrated by the fact that specifying the numerical value of the weight as 0·5 and maximizing the weighted sum of contributions to the two objectives, and maximizing aggregate or Transylvan consumption subject respectively to constraints on Transylvan consumption of Rs 10 crores and on aggregate consumption of Rs 6 crores, lead to the identical programme *t*. Of the three relevant items of information—the weight and the levels of performance with respect to the two objectives—only one need be specified in advance; the other two emerge from the optimization process. If we specify the weight as 0·5 and maximize the weighted sum, then diagrammatically we choose the programme that touches the highest *S*-line attainable of all the *S*-lines with slopes of —0·5. (The minus sign indicates that we are willing to *sacrifice* aggregate consumption for the sake of Transylvanistan.) This is illustrated in Figure 1.2.

We learn from the maximization process that the levels of Transylvan and aggregate consumption optimally consistent with the specified weight are Rs 10 crores and Rs 6 crores respectively. If instead of maximizing a weighted sum we specify a constraint of Rs 10 crores on Transylvan consumption (indicated by the vertical line labelled *U* in Figure 1.3), then we learn from Figure 1.3 that the corresponding maximum aggregate consumption attainable is Rs 6 crores and that the marginal trade-off between aggregate and Transylvan consumption, given by the slope of T at t, is 0·5.

Similarly, specification of Rs 6 crores as the minimum acceptable level of aggregate consumption (indicated by the horizontal line labelled V in Figure 1.4) generates a maximum

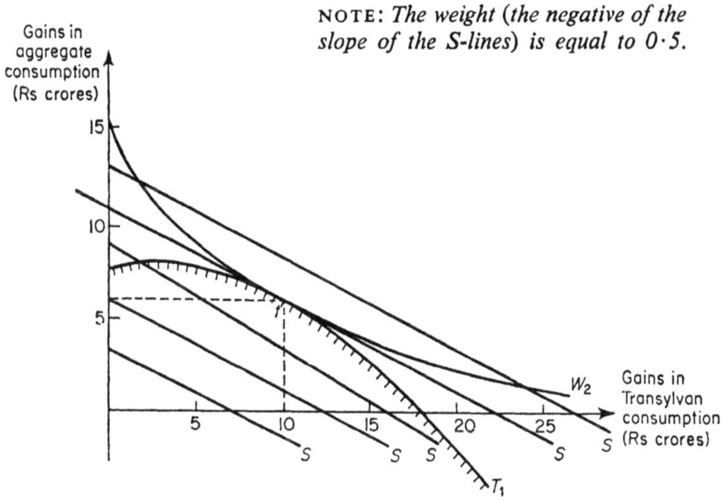

Figure 1.2. Maximization of a weighted sum of aggregate and Transylvan consumption

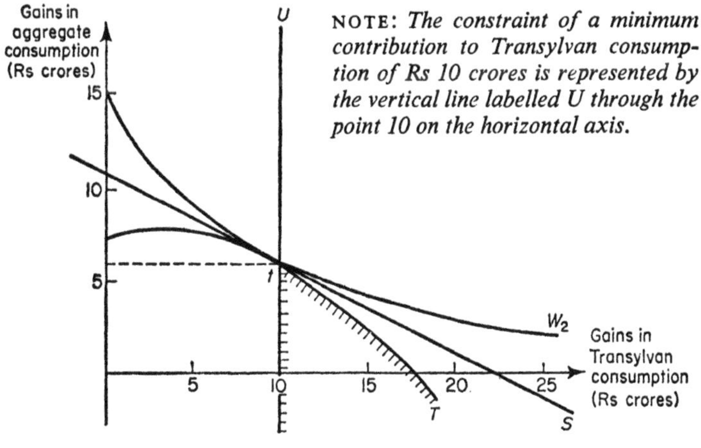

Figure 1.3. Constrained maximization of aggregate consumption

Transylvan consumption of Rs 10 crores and the same marginal trade-off of 0·5. This approach is illustrated in Figure 1.4.

The need for iterative determination of weights and constraint levels arises because policymakers cannot know the shape of the transformation function (T) in its entirety, nor can they be expected to articulate their preferences among alternative contributions of aggregate and Transylvan consumption

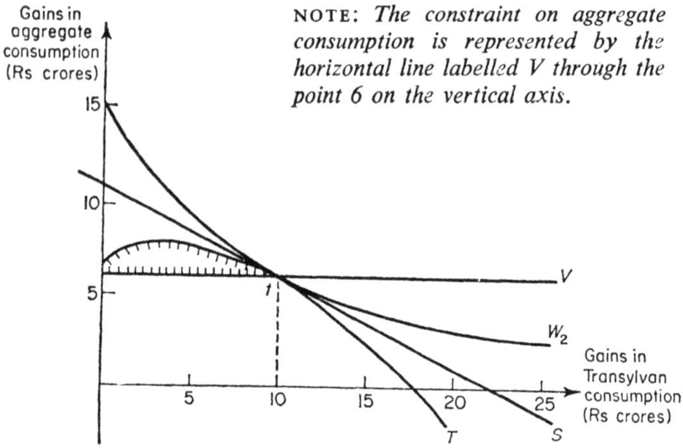

NOTE: *The constraint on aggregate consumption is represented by the horizontal line labelled V through the point 6 on the vertical axis.*

Figure 1.4. Constrained maximization of Transylvan consumption

in the form of a complete set of *W*-curves. Thus they can specify neither the marginal weight nor a performance level with confidence but must instead revise the weight or constraint level in the light of additional information about the range of feasible contributions of aggregate and Transylvan consumption that experimentation with the original choice of the weight or performance level generates. Suppose, for example, the weight is originally set at 0·33 rather than at 0·5; maximization of the weighted sum of aggregate and Transylvan consumption then leads to the programme t^*, with, as Figure 1.5 shows, aggregate consumption equal to Rs 7·5 crores and Transylvan consumption equal to Rs 7 crores. However, Figure 1.5 shows that the actual marginal weight for this combination—given by the negative of the slope of the desirability isoquant W^* through the point t^*—is 0·65. The difference between the actual marginal weight of 0·65 and the original choice of 0·33 suggests revision of the weight; the new weight to be employed in subsequent planning should lie between the extremes of 0·65 and 0·33.

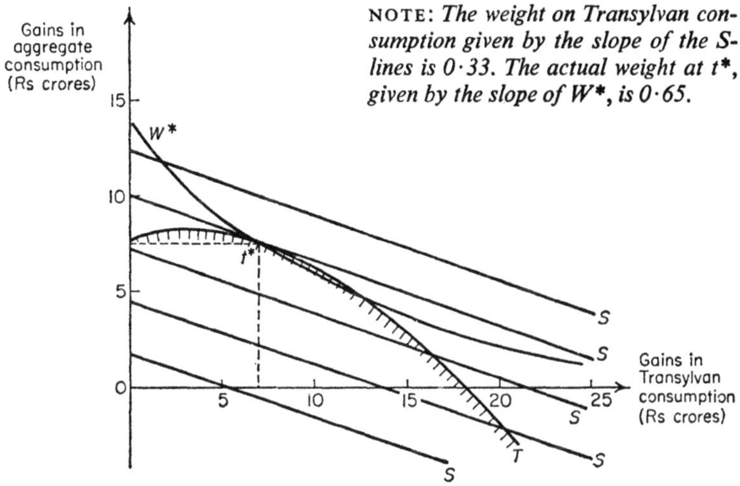

NOTE: *The weight on Transylvan consumption given by the slope of the S-lines is 0·33. The actual weight at t*, given by the slope of W*, is 0·65.*

Figure 1.5. Maximization of a weighted sum of aggregate and Transylvan consumption

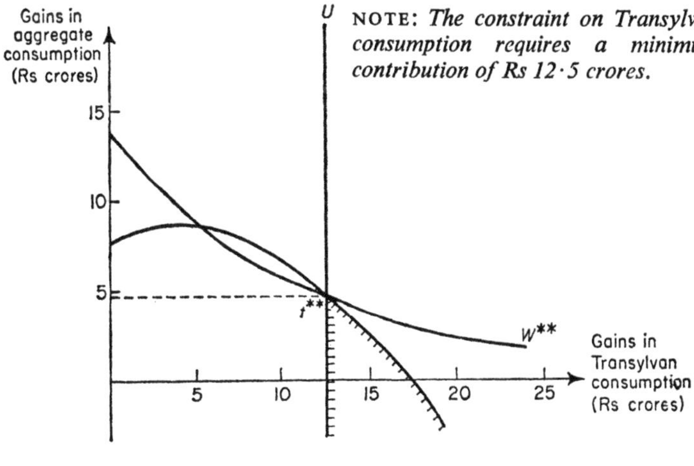

NOTE: *The constraint on Transylvan consumption requires a minimum contribution of Rs 12·5 crores.*

Figure 1.6. Constrained maximization of aggregate consumption

Suppose instead that a constraint on Transylvan consumption is initially set at Rs 12·5 crores. Then, as shown in Figure 1.6, maximization of aggregate consumption subject to this constraint produces the programme associated with the point t^{**}: Rs 4·5 crores of aggregate consumption and an implicit marginal weight, or marginal trade-off, of 0·67, representing the slope of the transformation function. The explicit marginal weight for the combination of Rs 12·5 crores of Transylvan consumption and Rs 4·5 crores of aggregate consumption is given by the slope of the desirability isoquant passing through this point, W^{**}, which is equal to $-0{\cdot}45$. Since at the margin the nation must give up Rs 6·7 of aggregate consumption to increase Transylvan consumption by Rs 10 and is willing to sacrifice only Rs 4·5 of aggregate consumption to do so, redistribution is, relatively speaking, expensive in terms of aggregate consumption. Consequently the constraint on Transylvan consumption should be revised downward in future investment planning. Alternatively, in the light of the information generated about the transformation function by constrained maximization, policymakers might find it convenient to shift from approach (1.2) to approach (1.1), that is, henceforth to specify the weight (somewhere between 0·67 and 0·45) and to direct planners to maximize the weighted sum of benefits.

It would be unnecessarily repetitive to work out the corresponding details of iteration in the approach specifying a constraint upon performance in terms of the aggregate consumption objective, for the discussion has already brought out the important points common to all approaches: first, that the optimum programme is characterized by the equality of the marginal weight on Transylvan consumption relative to aggregate consumption embodied in the desirability isoquants (W-curves) and the marginal trade-off embodied in the transformation function (T); second, that the differences between the marginal weights and the marginal trade-off that might characterize preliminary plans suggest to planners the direction that revision of plans ought to take.

The graphical analysis used to describe the three alternative approaches to the implementation of multiple objectives suggested earlier can also be used to illustrate other approaches.

For instance, solution of the conflict between regional redistribution of consumption and the level of aggregate consumption is sometimes posed in terms of "regional balance." In the terminology of this book regional balance means that aggregate consumption is to be maximized subject to the constraint that the ratio of Transylvan consumption gains to aggregate consumption gains exceeds a given fraction b. Symbolically this solution can be represented as

Max (net aggregate consumption gains)

subject to the constraint

$$\frac{\text{net Transylvan consumption gains}}{\text{net aggregate consumption gains}} \geqslant b. \qquad (1.4)$$

The optimization problem is shown graphically in Figure 1.7. Graphically b is represented by the tangent of the angle θ made

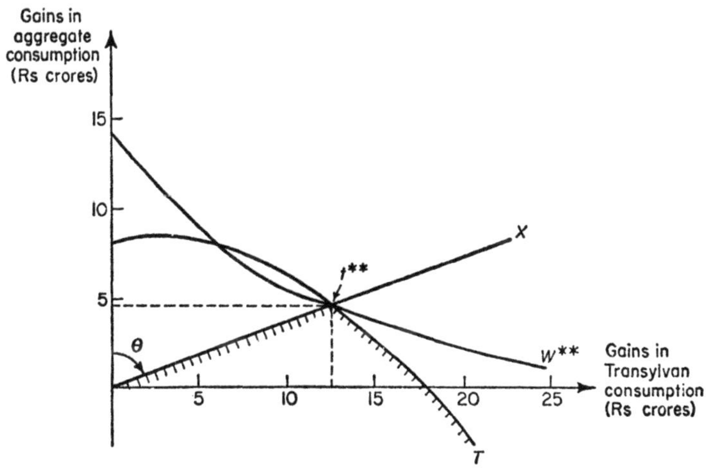

Figure 1.7. Maximization of aggregate consumption subject to a constraint on the ratio of Transylvan consumption to aggregate consumption

by the constraint ray X and the vertical axis, and for b equal to a hypothetical value of 2·78, the constraint of balance between Transylvan and aggregate gains leads to the investment programme t^{**}, providing Rs 12·5 crores to Transylvanistan and

Rs 4·5 crores of aggregate consumption. The nonoptimality of this programme is indicated by the inequality between the slope of the desirability isoquant W^{**} and the slope of the transformation function T. Since at the margin the nation is prepared to sacrifice less aggregate consumption for Transylvan consumption than it must do if the programme represented by t^{**} is put into effect, the constraint level b should be revised downward (that is, the constraint ray X should be rotated counterclockwise) to provide more aggregate consumption and less Transylvan consumption.

This discussion illustrates once again that constraint levels set without reference to the technological possibilities embodied in the transformation function will produce optimal investment programmes only by chance. If b happened to be set at the level represented by the angle θ in Figure 1.8, maximization constrained by the regional balance constraint represented by (1.4)

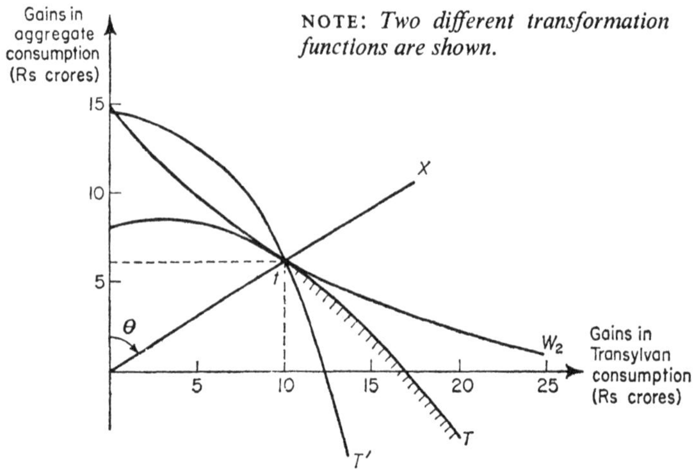

Figure 1.8. Maximization of aggregate consumption subject to a constraint on the ratio of Transylvan consumption to aggregate consumption

would lead to the investment programme t, the optimality of which is indicated by the equality of the slopes of T and W_2. But if the transformation function had the shape T' instead of T, the same choice of constraint level would lead to the same programme, which for the new transformation function would be nonoptimal.

Thus a regional balance constraint requiring, for example, that the ratio of regional consumption gains to aggregate gains be at least equal to the ratio of regional to total population or to any other magic but arbitrary number, can be optimal only by fortuitous conjunction with an appropriate transformation function.

The success of the approaches to planning outlined here depends critically on the assumption of *strict convexity* of the set of alternative feasible combinations of contributions to the several objectives of public policy. If the set of alternatives were not strictly convex, maximization of a weighted sum of benefits even with the appropriate marginal weight would not necessarily lead to the programme that optimally combines the two objectives.

Formally, a strictly convex set has the property that a straight line segment between any two points in the set lies wholly in the interior of the set. The existence of a strictly convex set in the present example is tantamount roughly to the existence of some complementarity between the aggregate and regional consumption objectives over the entire range of alternative investment programmes lying on T. In fact, the assumption of strictly convex sets of feasible policy alternatives is implicit throughout this study. (It appears again, for instance, in the "Time and Interest" section in Chapter 2.)

If the set of feasible combinations of aggregate consumption and Transylvan consumption delineated by T were convex but not strictly convex, line segments between points in the set would lie in the set but not necessarily in its interior, as shown in Figure 1.9, and maximization of a weighted sum of aggregate consumption and Transylvan consumption with the weights given by the slope of W_2 at t would fail to discriminate between t and all the nonoptimal points of T that fall in the range of T that coincides with S.

If the set of feasible combinations of aggregate consumption and Transylvan consumption delineated by T had the nonconvex shape shown in Figure 1.10, maximization of a weighted sum of benefits with the weight given by the common slope of W_3 and T at t would lead to the programme associated with t^{**}

rather than to the optimal programme associated with *t*. Moreover, iterative revision of a constraint on the basis of the

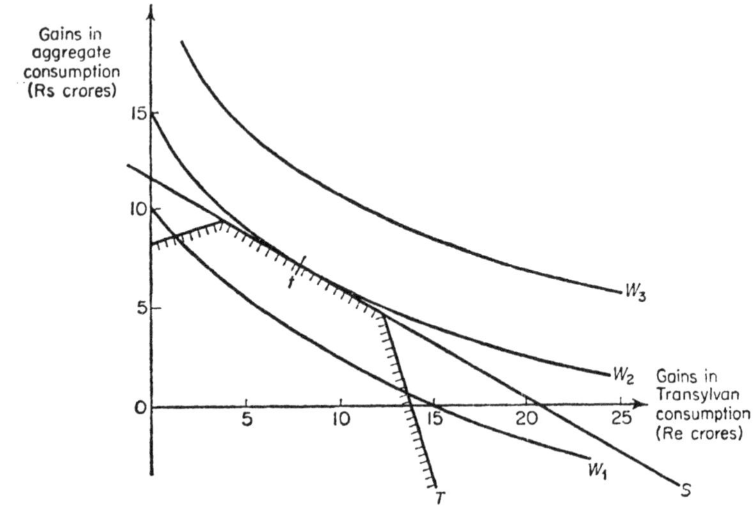

Figure 1.9. Convex (but not strictly convex) sets of feasible combinations

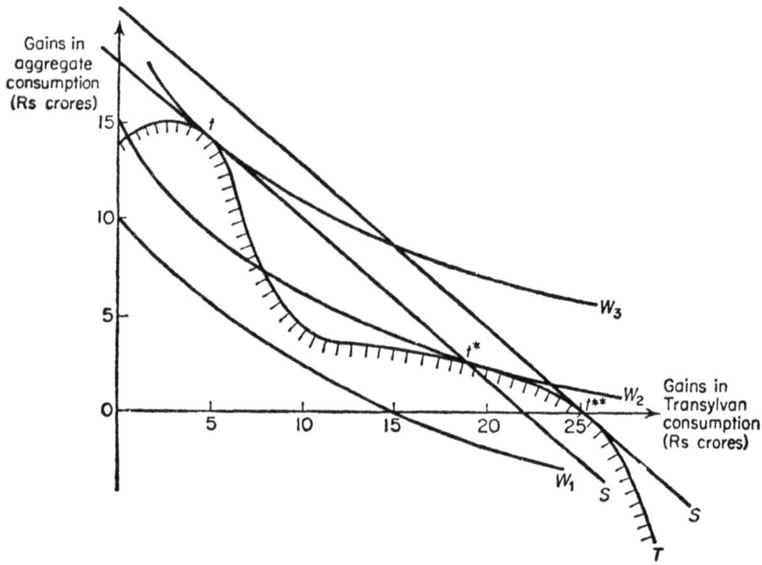

Figure 1.10. Nonconvex sets of feasible combinations

divergence between the explicit marginal weight and the marginal trade-off would not necessarily lead to the optimal investment programme. Iterative revision would lead to the optimal programme t if the iterative process were confined to a small enough neighbourhood of t, but otherwise iterative revision might lead to the nonoptimal programme t^*

Whether or not the transformation function exhibits the well-behaved form of Figures 1.1 to 1.8 or the ill-behaved form of Figures 1.9 and 1.10, implementation of multiple objectives requires a two-way flow of information between technicians designing public investment programmes and the policymakers setting the relative emphasis on objectives. I have implied that the iterative adjustment of weights or constraints can be reflected in modification of plans for individual projects, but the desirability of such refinement depends on the size and importance of the project in question and on the capacity of the planning process for revising plans with the requisite alacrity. In general a sequential iterative process of the following type would probably be preferable: The weights or constraints for new investment programmes might be revised periodically (for example, at the start of each five-year plan) to reflect information generated during the previous planning period.

The stress on the multiplicity of objectives that characterizes this study's approach to the choice of investment criteria for the public sector is at variance with the usual emphasis that economists give to the growth of aggregate consumption. Let me therefore make my position clear: My aim is simply to remove the aggregate consumption objective from the pedestal on which many would place it. The very terms in which aggregate consumption has been compared with other objectives of public policy indicate the bias: The "efficiency" objective, or sometimes simply the "economic" objective, is contrasted with "political" and "social" objectives in terms (and tones) that leave little doubt as to the second-class citizenship accorded to objectives other than maximization of aggregate consumption.

The labels "efficiency" and "economic" are especially unfortunate, for we are all against waste, and to emphasize "non-efficiency" or "non-economic" objectives sounds dangerously like favouring inefficiency and boondoggling. The problem is that the assumptions of most models of welfare economics preclude consideration of dimensions of welfare other than the size and distribution of consumption; moreover, the institutional bars to the attainment of desirable distributions of consumption are ignored. Hence (with one or two additional postulates) efficiency becomes equivalent to maximization of aggregate consumption;[1] it must be *assumed* that one begins from a desirable distribution of resources among the nation's citizens. Unfortunately, some economists base policy recommendations on conclusions drawn from abstract models, neglecting the differences between the models and the environment of actual decisions. This environment makes the single-minded pursuit of "efficiency"—in its particular meaning of maximization of aggregate consumption—an inadequate surrogate for maximization of national welfare.

Nor is the cause of systematic implementation of conflicting objectives helped by those more sophisticated economists who, recognizing the existence of a multiplicity of objectives, nevertheless throw up their hands at the idea of trying to attach relative weights to objectives other than aggregate consumption and therefore limit their attention to this last objective. The refusal on the part of so many economists to examine the relations between "efficiency" and "nonefficiency" objectives may go some way towards explaining why policymakers are so sceptical of economists' recommendations.

One final word. To stress the multiplicity of objectives is to stress the conflicts among them. The Indian Perspective Planning Division's (PPD) August 1962 discussion [*12*] of the implications of planning to abolish poverty by 1976, on the other hand, stresses the complementarity of objectives. The PPD hypothesizes that the distribution of income cannot be substantially modified[2] and that therefore "the attainment of a specified level of minimum income within a given period then

[1] The assumptions required for the identification of efficiency (Pareto optimality) with maximization of aggregate consumption are spelled out in Arthur Maass and others [*16*], pp. 20–58. If efficiency is interpreted not as Pareto-optimality but simply as a requirement that the public sector investment programme be designed so that additional gains towards any one goal are unobtainable except by reducing the performance of the programme with respect to other goals, then efficiency is itself the primary aim of the particular kind of benefit-cost analysis advocated in this book.

[2] [*12*], pp. 5 ff.

becomes purely a function of the rate of development."[1] Similarly Louis Lefeber's appendix on regional allocation and related problems[2] emphasizes the complementarity between increasing aggregate and regional consumption over the long run.

My own view is that although the broad strategy of development may be the same for a wide range of relative weights on the several goals of public policy, there are nevertheless conflicts among objectives at the tactical level of project planning that necessitate hard choices: What is good for the nation may *not* be good for Transylvanistan. However, having expressed this intuitive view, I should be the first to admit that I have little empirical knowledge of the extent to which the several goals of public policy actually are inconsistent: the extent to which regional and national goals conflict, the extent to which progress towards a more equal distribution of consumption conflicts with an increase in aggregate or regional consumption, or the extent to which progress towards self-sufficiency conflicts with increases in consumption or with a more equal distribution of consumption. Moreover, I doubt that I am alone in my ignorance. In short, quantitative study of the sensitivity of sectoral targets and project plans to the mix of objectives would undoubtedly be a most worthwhile expenditure of research time.

[1] [*12*], p. 7.
[2] Reprinted in [*13*], pp. 113–125, and in [*23*], pp. 18–29.

CHAPTER 2

SPECIFIC CRITERIA

Benefits

The goal of project design in the public sector may be stated as maximization of net benefits subject to constraints, but once it is decided to explicitly reflect the multiplicity of objectives in project planning it becomes impossible to speak of a project's benefits without relating benefits to a particular objective or a weighted sum of objectives. Hence in defining benefits each objective will be considered in turn.

Aggregate consumption benefits are the increments in consumption a project provides, valued in terms of individuals' willingness to pay. This definition, to be sure, presents several problems. First, the majority of the goods and services produced in the public sector are not directly consumed by individuals; irrigation and fertilizers, for instance, are intermediate products in the production of food and fibre as well as of other intermediates. However, this is not an insurmountable problem in the measurement of aggregate consumption benefits. Producers' willingness to pay for goods and services can in general be taken as a measure of their value to ultimate consumers, and this willingness to pay can be measured by the residual remaining after deducting from the value of producers' outputs (for example, sugar cane) the costs of all inputs (land, labour services, and others) save the publicly provided ones (irrigation and fertilizer) whose benefits we seek to measure.[1] But a sizable fraction of the goods and services emanating from the public sector neither are consumed directly nor are inputs to the production of consumer goods. Steel, for example, is not consumed directly, and in India only a small fraction of the available supply is utilized in the fabrication of consumer goods. The aggregate consumption benefits from additional

[1] The difference between the value of outputs and the costs of inputs other than the publicly provided ones is the economic "rent" earned on the inputs coming from the public sector.

steel production are the increments to *future* consumption provided by the factories, machinery, transport equipment, and the like built with steel.[1]

Note the emphasis on *willingness to pay* in my definition. It is users' *willingness* to pay rather than what they might *actually* pay that is the measure of aggregate consumption benefits. Willingness to pay will exceed actual payments for the output of a public project whenever (1) the good or service is rationed, formally or informally, by any means other than price, or (2) the output represents more than a marginal increment in the total supply of the good or service, and perfect price discrimination is not employed in the distribution of the output. To say that willingness to pay rather than actual payments is the appropriate measure of benefits is not to say the pricing policies employed by public enterprises have no effect on aggregate consumption. It is the willingness to pay of the actual users that is relevant; consequently pricing policies which deprive users with the highest willingness to pay in favour of users with lower willingness to pay reduce aggregate consumption benefits. This accounts for economists' preoccupation with the price which just brings demand into line with supply, that is, the price which just clears a competitive market; price rationing directs publicly produced goods and services to those uses which make the greatest contribution to aggregate consumption. If the market-clearing price—say P_0—is charged and all are free to buy as much or as little as they please at this price, then enlightened self-interest will lead each to buy until the direct or indirect contribution to consumption of the last unit purchased falls to P_0. Thus all uses for which someone is willing to pay at least P_0 will be undertaken, and all uses for which no one is willing to pay P_0 will be foregone. Price thus acts as an impersonal and objective rationing device, ensuring that goods and

[1] Needless to say, the entire annual increment to consumption from a machine is not due to the steel; it is the *marginal* annual consumption increment per additional ton of steel that is the benefit of a ton of steel. Unfortunately the willingness to pay for a ton of steel devoted to fabrication of plant and equipment is not in general an adequate measure of the value of the future consumption stream generated because, for a variety of reasons, the social and private evaluations of the future relative to the present may differ. This point is discussed later in this chapter under the heading "Time and Interest."

services end up in the uses for which willingness to pay is greatest. In principle, rationing by means other than price can accomplish this goal, but the administrative problems are formidable. If the price is less than P_0, then the quantity demanded will in general exceed the supply, and the windfall that accrues to the lucky recipients gives an incentive for misrepresentation of willingness to pay. Enlightened self-interest cannot be harnessed to the allocation of the available supply unless the price is set in such a manner that self-interest becomes self-enforcing. Nevertheless, there are, as will be seen on pp. 88–92, goals of pricing policy that conflict with the allocational goal so ably served by the policy of charging the market clearing price. These goals may make it worthwhile to take on the formidable administrative task of rationing publicly provided goods and services. Thus the distinctions among aggregate consumption benefits (willingness to pay), competitive market value, and financial returns are real and important.

The relations among willingness to pay, competitive market value, consumers' surplus, and actual payments can be illustrated graphically. The curve *DEF* in Figure 2.1 shows the quantity of irrigation water that cultivators would demand at different prices, abstracting from such important aspects of irrigation as the time of delivery and the quality of water.

The willingness to pay for any particular quantity—for example, Q_0—is approximated by the entire area under the demand curve OQ_0ED.[1] It is equal to the sum of competitive market value, the rectangle OQ_0EP_0, and consumers' surplus, the triangle P_0ED. Willingness to pay for irrigation is equal to the value of additional production from irrigation or, in other

[1] The reasons why the area under the demand curve is only an approximation to willingness to pay are too technical to go into here. Suffice it to say that for projects producing consumers' goods, the area under the demand curve may be a bad approximation to willingness to pay if consumers' willingness to pay is a large fraction of their total incomes. Sir John Hicks [*11*], Chapter 2, especially pp. 38–41, and Milton Friedman [*10*], pp. 47–99, explore the technical aspects of the relationship between the demand curve and willingness to pay for consumers' goods. (The problem of divergence between the area under the demand curve and willingness to pay does not arise in the case of producers' goods. The area under the demand curve of a profit maximizing producer is exactly equal to his willingness to pay.)

words, from the increase in income that farmers would derive from irrigation, net of any extra costs for additional inputs. The competitive market value, on the other hand, is equal to the product $P_0 \times Q_0$, where P_0 is the competitive price of irrigation associated with the quantity Q_0, that is, the price at which cultivators would purchase exactly Q_0 units of water if free to buy as much as they liked at this price.[1]

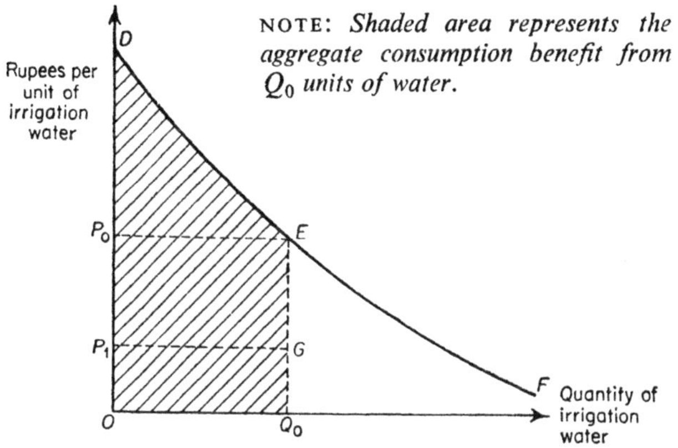

Figure 2.1. Demand for irrigation, willingness to pay, consumers' surplus, competitive market value, and actual payments

The actual payment may differ from both willingness to pay and the competitive market value. In Figure 2.1 a price of only P_1 is assumed so that the actual payment of cultivators totals $P_1 \times Q_0$, given by the area OQ_0GP_1. Of course the price P_1 would require the irrigation authority to resort to nonprice rationing in the distribution of water if Q_0 units were the total available supply; at all prices below P_0 cultivators would attempt to use more than Q_0 units of water. Indeed, in India and elsewhere actual payments for canal water generally run much

[1] A frequently encountered objection to defining aggregate consumption benefits in terms of willingness to pay is the difficulty of measuring the demand curve. The objection is only superficially valid, however, since estimation of the demand curve is just as necessary to measure benefits by means of the more conventional definition in terms of competitive market values. The difference lies in the use to which the demand curve is put, not in its measurement. On this point see Christopher Foster [9], pp. 139–149.

lower than the competitive market value, not to mention willingness to pay, and nonprice rationing is a familiar part of water distribution.[1]

Redistribution benefits are the consumption gains of particular groups or regions. As for the aggregate consumption objective, the basis of the valuation of goods and services is individual preference. However, unlike the aggregate consumption objective, with respect to which pricing policy is simply an indirect instrumental variable, for redistribution objectives the level of project revenues is a direct determinant of benefits:

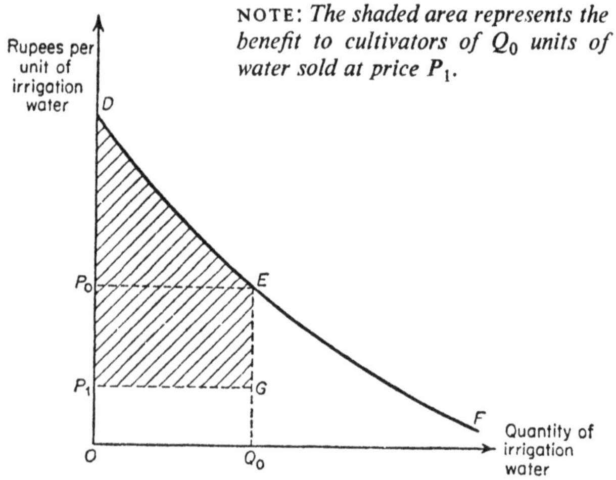

Figure 2.2. Demand for irrigation, benefits to cultivators, and actual payments

The gains to a particular group of project users are the *difference* between their willingness to pay and the actual charges levied upon them.

Redistribution benefits can be clearly contrasted with aggregate consumption benefits by means of the irrigation demand schedule of Figure 2.1, reproduced above in Figure 2.2. Once again the quantity Q_0 and the price P_1 are assumed to hold. The benefits to cultivators as a group are given by the shaded area

[1] Aggregate consumption benefits are discussed in greater detail in Arthur Maass and others [*16*], pp. 20–62, under the heading "The Efficiency Objective."

P_1GED, which represents the difference between willingness to pay (OQ_0ED) and actual payments (OQ_0GP_1).[1]

Merit-want benefits are the quantitative contribution of projects to the output of the specific consumer goods and services that public policy has elevated above tests based on market prices, that is, on individual willingness to pay. For example, suppose nutrition is singled out as a merit want. Nutritional benefits can be measured as a vector of calories, fats, proteins, and other components deemed essential to an adequate diet. Premiums which policymakers impose explicitly (or implicitly, by means of constraints) determine merit-want values in the same way that market prices determine marginal aggregate consumption values in competitive markets.

The definition of *self-sufficiency benefits* varies with the meaning accorded to self-sufficiency. If the trade-balance definition is employed, the contribution of a particular programme or project to this objective is measured by adding (1) the value of exports that the project makes possible to (2) the value of imports for which project outputs or derivatives substitute, and subtracting from this sum (3) the value of imports—on current as well as capital account—that the project necessitates. If self-sufficiency means autarky, then export benefits are dropped from the previous definition.[2]

Costs

The meaning of costs, like the meaning of benefits, depends on the objective: Costs and benefits are simply two sides of the same coin. As benefits measure the contribution of a programme to an objective, so costs measure the extent to which activities that the programme displaces elsewhere in the economy would contribute to the objective.

Thus in a perfectly functioning competitive economy, money outlays measure the *aggregate consumption* costs of a project. But market prices are not appropriate measures of what the economy forgoes if the competitive assumptions do not hold. A

[1] Redistribution benefits are also discussed extensively in Maass and others [*16*], pp. 62–86.

[2] See Chenery [*4*], pp. 87–93, for a more detailed discussion of self-sufficiency benefits.

relevant example is the evaluation of labour costs. The money wage is not the correct measure of loss of aggregate consumption elsewhere in the economy if it does not reflect the marginal productivity of labour. This *caveat* about the use of the wage rate to measure the cost of labour might be interpreted as an injunction to evaluate all labour employed in public investment at a zero "shadow-wage" rate in view of the widespread unemployment and underemployment in India. But such an interpretation is not warranted. First, much of the labour employed in public capital formation is of a skilled nature that, despite widespread unemployment, is in short supply. Second, with respect to those labour categories in which large-scale unemployment does exist, political considerations may make it impossible to utilize taxation or inflation to the extent necessary to drive the marginal productivity of labour in the public sector to zero. In the event political constraints limit the mobilization of unemployed labour, the social opportunity cost of labour or "shadow wage" is not equal to the (zero) marginal productivity of unemployed labour. Instead, if the real wage of unskilled labour is institutionally fixed at a level w, and the entire wage is consumed, then in terms of the aggregate consumption objective the shadow wage becomes $\theta\ (\rho/\bar{r} - 1)w$. θ is the amount by which one rupee of public investment reduces private investment; $(\rho/\bar{r} - 1)$ is the difference between the social value of one rupee of private investment $(\rho/\bar{r})$ and the social value of each rupee of consumption (1) afforded public sector workers by new employment. (Both θ and $\rho/\bar{r}$ are discussed in the following section, "Time and Interest.") Optimally, employment in the public sector is increased until its marginal productivity is brought into equality with the shadow wage—if the aggregate consumption objective is controlling.

Labour is not the only item whose market price may differ from the social value of alternative uses. A rapid transformation of the economy, which must accompany a high rate of growth of aggregate output, of itself produces discrepancies between market price and social costs. Fortunately we need not despair of identifying these discrepancies. One purpose of specifying output targets by commodities in quinquennial and perspective plans should be to provide estimates of the social costs of the inputs to public sector projects by means of the "shadow prices" implicit in the plan.

Costs with respect to *redistributional objectives* are the sacrifices that the particular groups or regions in question bear in the implementation of redistributional goals, for example, the share of project costs that are levied as taxes on non-beneficiaries within a region to which income is supposed to be redistributed. (The costs borne by beneficiaries are already deducted from their willingness to pay in computing redistribution benefits.)

Merit-want costs exist only if the public project requires a sacrifice with respect to the merit want in question in order to realize the merit-want goal.

Self-sufficiency costs of a public sector project or programme are reflected in its direct foreign exchange requirements.

Time and Interest

The benefits of a programme or project with respect to all objectives are realized over a long period of time, and, from the vantage point of the present, benefits are not equally valuable at all future dates. If development takes place as planned, the Indian economy will be farther along the road to fulfilment of all objectives with the completion of each five-year plan. Hence one need accept only the assumption of diminishing marginal utility to agree that, from the point of view of the present, equal increments of benefits are less desirable, the longer the economy must wait to reap them.

The problem of comparing benefits occurring in different years is much like the problem of comparing benefits with respect to different objectives: Either relative weights must be placed on benefits at different times and the weighted sum maximized or constraints must be placed on programme performance at different times (in which case weights are implicit in the level of the constraints). The percentage rate at which the weight on benefits—either explicit or implicit—changes over time is called the *interest* or *discount rate*. The discount rate may be different for each objective.

We consider first the aggregate consumption objective.[1]

[1] As an aid in clarifying the problem of the intertemporal criterion, I

An intertemporal criterion for aggregate consumption. The aggregate consumption objective can be looked at as a set of objectives: If the government judges that contributions to aggregate consumption in different years are, at the margin, of different value—presumably less important in each succeeding year because the economy is expected to become richer—then contributions to aggregate consumption generated by a project become a weighted sum,

$$\sum_{t=1}^{\infty} \lambda_t B_t(x) - \lambda_0 K(x) \tag{2.1}$$

where

1. x represents the "scale" of the public programme whose design is in question.[1]
2. t represents time (in years),
3. $B_t(x)$ represents the net addition to aggregate consumption from a project of scale x in year t,
4. $K(x)$ represents domestic capital cost (assumed for simplicity to take place at once) as a function of scale,
5. λ_t represents the relative weight on consumption in year t.

The discount rate for year t, r_t, is related to the weights upon benefits in successive years by the formula

$$r_t = \frac{\lambda_t - \lambda_{t+1}}{\lambda_{t+1}}$$

That is, r_t represents the (percentage) rate at which the weight on aggregate consumption falls over time. Customarily we assume that r_t is constant over time—largely through ignorance, since there is no logical reason why it should be expected to remain constant. And normally we fix λ_0, the weight on present

shall assume that policymakers have opted for explicit weighting of benefits over time. This is not really a restrictive assumption, for the logic of time-weighting is the same regardless of whether the weights are explicit or implicit, and this assumption has much to commend it in that it permits simplifying the problem of intertemporal choice by framing it at one of choosing a discount rate.

[1] "Scale" is in quotation marks because in general it is necessary to describe an investment programme or project in more than the single dimension or size. That is, x is more realistically thought of as a vector than as a scalar description.

consumption, at unity; present consumption is the unit of account, the standard of reference against which we compare all other benefits and costs. With these conventions we may drop the t subscript from r_t and write λ_t as $(1 + r)^{-t}$. Thus (2.1) becomes

$$\sum_{t=1}^{\infty} \frac{B_t(x)}{(1 + r)^t} - K(x) \tag{2.2}$$

In this form the weighted sum of aggregate consumption is usually called the *net present value* of aggregate consumption benefits; the choice of weights now becomes a choice of discount rate.

Recasting the problem of choosing intertemporal weights in the form of choosing a discount rate is but a formal transformation; the problem of choosing the discount rate is a formidable one and an important one. There are many projects and project increments which show a positive net present value of aggregate consumption benefits at a discount rate of, say, 5%, but fail to pass muster at 10%. Which discount rate is appropriate? If the analogy between comparing contributions to a single objective at different points in time and comparing contributions to distinct objectives at a single point in time is an apt analogy, then there would seem to be no way to resolve the problem of choosing a discount rate for aggregate consumption that escapes the need for value judgments. Just as policy makers must articulate relative weights on distinct objectives like aggregate consumption and redistribution, so must they articulate their views about the rate at which the weight on marginal contributions to aggregate consumption ought to decline with time. In order to avoid these value judgments, it has been widely suggested that the aggregate consumption benefits of public sector projects be discounted at a rate of interest equal to the marginal internal rate of return (r^*) in the private sector.[1] If only those project or programme incre-

[1] The internal rate of return of an investment is defined as the discount rate at which the present value of return minus costs is zero. In our terminology, the internal rate of return is that value of r for which

$$\sum_{t=1}^{\infty} \frac{B_t(x)}{(1+ r)^t} - K(x)$$

is equal to zero. The marginal internal rate of return is equivalent to

ments are undertaken whose present value at the discount rate r^* is positive, then (and only then)—according to the proponents of this procedure—all investment undertaken in the public sector will yield a time-weighted contribution to aggregate consumption as great as that afforded by private sector investments.

The usual basis for the choice of r^* as the public sector discount rate is that it reflects a balancing of individuals' marginal time preferences in consumption with the marginal productivity of investment opportunities available to the economy. The weakness of this basis of choice is that individuals' intertemporal preferences for collective decisions may differ from the preferences that they express in private investment decisions; for reasons discussed in an earlier paper of mine [*20*], even a perfect capital market may be inadequate to enable individuals to express all the relevant properties of their feelings about the intertemporal distribution of consumption.

This failure of capital markets would not be very important if the government were in the position *vis-à-vis* the private sector that an individual decision-maker is *vis-à-vis* a perfect capital market, as is sometimes assumed implicitly in an alternative justification of the use of r^* as the public sector discount rate. Irving Fisher was able to show that with a perfect capital market each individual can attain the most gratifying consumption programme available to him by choosing the investment programme that maximizes the present value of his investment at the market rate of interest, then borrowing or lending at the market rate of interest according to his subjective intertemporal preferences in consumption [*8*]. The beauty of this procedure is that it is only in the second stage of his decision process—the borrowing or lending decision—that the individual's subjective intertemporal preferences enter the picture. He chooses his consumption and investment programmes independently, and the latter *without* reference to his personal intertemporal preferences.

The government, however, is *not* in the position relative to the private sector that Irving Fisher's decision-maker is relative to

Keynes' marginal efficiency of capital. See Armen Alchian [*1*]. There are technical difficulties associated with the internal rate of return, but these need not detain us. See Pierre Massé [*21*], Chapter 1, especially pp. 20–29.

the capital market. The individual may be able to utilize the borrowing-lending mechanism to distribute consumption over time in accordance with his subjective preferences, but no analogous mechanism is available to the government. The government cannot ensure that the aggregate consumption benefits of a public investment programme are reinvested at a rate of return equal to r^* to provide consumption in the time pattern desired by the government, the logical equivalent of a private decision-maker's lending the returns of an investment at the market rate of interest to redistribute the returns toward the future. Nor is there a mechanism by which the government can, like a private decision-maker, "borrow" consumption against the security of future benefits. In other words, the Government of India is not today, nor will it be in the forseeable future, in a position to attain the optimal mix of consumption and investment independently of its choice of public sector projects. The Government of India cannot simply assume that it can compensate for differences between the actual time pattern of returns from public projects and the desired time pattern of consumption by bringing about changes in the mix of private consumption and investment through fiscal and monetary policies. India has not been able to raise the rate of domestic savings much beyond 10%; yet few would dare claim that India has achieved an optimal rate of saving. Indeed, if fiscal and monetary policies were themselves powerful enough to bring about the mix of private consumption and investment that the Government of India desires, there would be relatively little need for the elaborate direction and control embodied in the five year plans.

Up to now we have accepted the contention that r^* really does reflect productive opportunities, and our criticism has been moulded within this framework. In fact in any economy, and more especially in an underdeveloped economy like India, there are good grounds for supposing that departures from the textbook assumption of competition—in labour and product markets as well as in the capital market—are significant enough to create a gap between private profits and net increments to consumption even at the margin and hence significant enough to divorce r^* from the marginal rate of return of aggregate consumption (sometimes called the "social rate of return"). For example, the private returns on which r^* is based are revenues and money costs, but the contribution of private investment to aggregate consumption depends on willingness to pay and social costs. If a private investment adds more than a marginal amount to the supply of a product in any particular market, and the market is competitive, the difference between willingness to pay and revenue will be equal to the consumers' surplus on the increment to supply. (Also, private returns do not reflect indirect consumption gains, about which more will be said later in this chapter under the heading "Secondary Benefits.") Moreover, any gap between the prices and marginal productivities of resources results in a difference between money and social costs. An important example is the gap between the wage and the marginal productivity of labour, which is bound to exist in situations of widespread underemployment and unemployment.

In recognition of these imperfections it is sometimes suggested that the marginal rate of return of consumption (or marginal social rate of return) provided by private investment, rather than the marginal rate of return of profits (r^*), is the appropriate discount rate for public investment if the two rates differ. The assumption implicit in this suggestion is that the marginal rate of return of consumption from private investment is equal to, and a surrogate for, the marginal rate of discount emerging from individuals' intertemporal consumption preferences. But this is tantamount to asserting that the over-all rate of investment in the economy is optimal, and it is hard to see how one could accept the existence of a discrepancy between the private rate of return, r^*, and the social rate of return and still argue that capital markets optimally balance "opportunity" and "impatience"—quite apart from the theoretical objections raised in reference [*20*] to the capital market as a device for registering intertemporal preferences.

Alternatively, one could base acceptance of the social rate of return on the contention that the Fisherian relationship of an individual to the capital market is an appropriate analogy for the relationship of the government to the private sector. But it seems to me that to state this contention is to refute it; to apply the Fisherian relationship of the individual to the market to the role of the government in a mixed economy is to assume implicitly that the government can achieve an optimal mix of consumption and investment, and this without sacrificing any output for the sake of the mix.

The conclusion that emerges from this discussion is that the government cannot divorce investment decisions from decisions about the time pattern of consumption and therefore cannot escape making a judgment as to the relative value of benefits at different times in the formulation of investment criteria. Nor can the government infer an appropriate rate of discount for comparing the present value of the benefits of public investment with the present value of the alternative use of resources from rates of return of either revenues or consumption unless the government is prepared to judge the over-all rate of investment in the economy to be optimal. Otherwise the appropriate rate of discount, which we shall call $\bar{r}$, can be inferred only from the intertemporal consumption preferences that the government holds as proxy for the people.

If the aggregate consumption objective were the sole determinant of public policy, it would be true (and consistent with the argument of the preceding paragraphs) that all investment opportunities—public and private—for which the present value of aggregate consumption at the discount rate $\bar{r}$ is positive should be exploited. In this case both the marginal rate of return of consumption from public investment and the marginal consumption return from private investment (but not necessarily the private rate of return r^*) would equal the marginal rate of discount $\bar{r}$. But the existence of objectives that conflict with maximization of aggregate consumption prevent single-minded devotion to this goal. Moreover, aside from conflicting objectives, political constraints such as those that prevent the complete mobilization of unskilled labour[1] limit the government's ability to carry public and private investment to the point where marginal rates of return of aggregate consumption in both sectors equal the marginal rate of discount $\bar{r}$.

In this case the over-all rate of investment in the economy will not be optimal, and we can give at best very limited guidance to the relationship between $\bar{r}$ and observable rates of capital productivity: $\bar{r}$ will be greater or smaller than the marginal rate of return of consumption to investment according to

[1] See pp. 69–70, especially note 1 on p. 70.

whether the over-all rate of investment is judged smaller or greater than optimal in terms of the aggregate consumption objective. (Even this little cannot be said about the relationship between $\bar{r}$ and r^*.)

The independence in nonoptimal situations of the social rate of discount $\bar{r}$ from rates of return on private investment of both consumption and revenues does not imply that private sector returns are irrelevant in the formulation of the intertemporal criterion for public investment. Investment outlays in the public and private sectors are not independent of one another, and when the availability of capital goods is as severely limited as in India, expansion of public investment generally must lead to some contraction of private investment, at least in the short run. And the present value of the sacrifice of future aggregate consumption entailed in the contraction of private investment is not accurately reflected in the market price of capital goods if the marginal rate of return of aggregate consumption from private investment differs from the marginal social rate of discount. In this case the nominal value of public investment funds of Re 1·00 per rupee must be replaced by a shadow price (or "opportunity cost") reflecting the present value, evaluated at the social rate of discount, of the consumption stream that the alternative private use of one rupee's worth of inputs to public investment would generate.[1] If the objective is stated as maximization of a weighted sum of aggregate consumption over time, the objective function (2.2) must be rewritten as

$$\sum_{t=1}^{\infty} \frac{B_t(x)}{(1+\bar{r})^t} - aK(x), \qquad (2.3)$$

where $\bar{r}$ represents the marginal social rate of discount, and a represents the opportunity cost per rupee of public investment.

To compute the numerical value of a, two questions must be answered: What portion of the resources required to undertake public investment comes from the private investment sector?

[1] One interpretation of the objective of socialism (one, I might add, that I believe confuses ends and means) is that consumption valued at one rupee by individuals is more desirable socially if emanating from public enterprise rather than private enterprise. The extent that the shadow price of public investment funds fails to reflect displacement of private investment might be taken as a measure of the weight attached to this interpretation of socialism.

What is the present value of the stream of aggregate consumption benefits that the displaced private investment would generate? To spell out the answers in some detail, let us retreat to the safety of a simplified model.

Suppose that the aggregate consumption generated by private investment is a perpetual stream whose annual magnitude is ρ per cent of the original outlay. The parameter ρ is the social rate of return to private investment, that is, the rate of return of aggregate consumption to private investment; if aggregate consumption benefits coincide with private returns, then ρ is equal to the private rate of return r^*.

Suppose also that the amount of private investment displaced by each rupee of public investment is θ. This parameter is restricted by the inequality $0 \leqslant \theta \leqslant 1$. For the time being, assume full employment of resources so that the portion of resources required to undertake public investment that does not come out of private investment must come out of private consumption.

With these assumptions the shadow price of public investment funds is

$$a = \theta \frac{\rho}{\bar{r}} + (1 - \theta), \tag{2.4}$$

where $\rho/\bar{r}$ represents the present value of the perpetual stream of consumption of ρ rupees per year evaluated at the marginal social rate of discount $\bar{r}$; $\theta\ \rho/\bar{r}$ consequently represents the loss from displacement of private investment occasioned by each rupee of public investment. The second term $(1 - \theta)$ is the portion of each rupee of public investment that displaces private consumption; this portion is reckoned at face value because the unit of account is present consumption.

Equation (2.4) defines the minimum benefit-cost ratio (more precisely, the minimum ratio of the present value of benefits to capital outlays) that an increment to a public sector programme must show to qualify for inclusion if the aggregate consumption objective is the sole criterion of the programme's composition. If, for example, $\bar{r} = 0{\cdot}05$, $\rho = 0{\cdot}10$, and $\theta = 0{\cdot}90$, then $a = 1{\cdot}90$. That is, increments to public investment programmes must show a present value per rupee of outlay in excess of the cutoff benefit-cost ratio of Rs $1{\cdot}90$ per rupee rather than simply meet the easier test of a cutoff benefit-cost ratio of unity.

Two remarks are in order here. First, the greater the extent to which public investment draws on resources otherwise employed in the production of consumer goods, the lower is the numerical value of θ. Under the assumption that the community's weight on the future relative to the present is greater than the private market's weight, it is clearly advantageous to design monetary and fiscal policies to minimize the reduction of private investment in response to expansion of investment in the public sector.

Second, in so far as public investment can draw on resources that would otherwise be idle, its opportunity costs may be smaller. In the event public investment partially mobilizes slack, the formula for opportunity cost (2.4) must be replaced by the formula

$$a = \theta \frac{\rho}{\bar{r}} + \theta^*,$$

where θ represents, as before, the amount of private investment displaced by each rupee of public investment, θ^* represents displaced private consumption, and $1 - (\theta + \theta^*)$ represents the extent to which each rupee of public investment draws upon otherwise slack resources. θ^* may even be negative; public investment may increase rather than decrease private consumption. Consider the surplus-labour situation to which allusion was made on p. 46. Suppose in response to rural unemployment, the government undertakes labour intensive public works, paying each worker a real wage w. If each worker tries to consume his entire wage, his demand for wage goods will increase by w. If this demand is to be met, either consumption goods must be transferred from the rest of the economy to the newly employed or resources must be shifted from private investment to production of additional consumption goods. To the extent rural public works simply transfer consumption goods, their opportunity cost in terms of aggregate consumption is zero. But suppose that only a fraction $(1 - \theta)$ of the consumption demands of newly employed workers is met by transferring consumption goods from elsewhere in the economy; the remainder, θ, must then be met by substituting production of consumption goods for private investment. Thus the net effect of public works will be to reduce private investment by θ and to increase private consumption by the same amount. The opportunity cost of one worker, the "shadow wage," becomes

$$w^* = \left(\theta\frac{\rho}{\bar{r}} + \theta^*\right)w = \left(\theta\frac{\rho}{\bar{r}} - \theta\right)w = \theta\left(\frac{\rho}{\bar{r}} - 1\right)w.$$

This is the result stated without elaboration on p. 46. It is noteworthy that the shadow wage w^* in this case may be greater than the market wage w, although with the parameter values $\bar{r} = 0{\cdot}05$, $\rho = 0{\cdot}10$, and $\theta = 0{\cdot}90$, w^* turns out to be equal to $0{\cdot}90w$.

This discussion of the measurement of opportunity costs is largely a summary of a model that I presented in the *Quarterly Journal of Economics* [*19*]. Although the formal model itself makes many simplifications, it includes many aspects of reality that I shall only touch on here. Reinvestment in both the public and private sectors, for example, is a critical issue, but I have sidestepped it by assuming that both ρ and $B_t(x)$ represent consumption rather than income flows. Differences in reinvestment of income between the public and private sectors may, however, be as important as the displacement of one sector's investment by the other's.

To illustrate the complications arising from reinvestment, consider the problem of benefit evaluation raised in note 1 on page 41. A public (or private) sector steel plant, let us suppose, produces a ton of steel that is used to augment private investment in plant and equipment. The benefit from the ton of steel is not fully reflected in the private investor's willingness to pay for steel since his willingness to pay mirrors the present value of the consumption stream generated by the steel at the marginal *private* rate of discount. The correct basis for evaluation of steel used in investment is the present value at the marginal *social* rate of discount of the consumption stream the steel generates.

This point can be elaborated by means of simple algebra. Under the simplifying assumption $\rho = r^*$, a private investor's willingness to pay p rupees for a ton of steel reflects a perpetual consumption stream whose annual value is p times the marginal rate of return in the private sector ρ. The present value of this perpetuity at the social rate of discount $\bar{r}$ is the annual value of the perpetuity divided by the discount rate $\bar{r}$, or $p(\rho/\bar{r})$. In other words, the aggregate consumption benefit from the production of capital goods is $\rho/\bar{r}$ times the private willingness to pay.

In general, if a constant proportion μ of an output of a public (or private) sector investment is an input to private capital formation, and the remainder $(1 - \mu)$ is immediately consumed, then the aggregate consumption benefit of one unit of output is given by the shadow price

$$\left[\mu \frac{\rho}{\bar{r}} + (1 - \mu)\right]p,$$

where p represents the price private individuals of firms are willing to pay for the unit of output. The value of μ will vary among outputs; for example, I should expect μ to be higher for steel than for irrigation. So long as $\bar{r}$ is less than ρ it is clearly in the interest of the aggregate consumption objective for public sector projects to produce goods and services that are technologically suited to further investment rather than consumption, and for which μ is of necessity close to unity. For the higher the value of μ, the more private willingness to pay undervalues a good or service and the less likely the private sector is to produce the good or service in adequate measure.[1] Similarly, in so far as choice exists, the aggregate consumption objective dictates pricing and distribution policies that place public sector outputs in the hands of private investors rather than private consumers and so leads to a high value of μ. In addition, provided the marginal propensity to invest revenue in the public sector is higher than the marginal propensity to invest income in the private sector, reinvestment considerations dictate prices for publicly produced outputs as high as the "traffic will bear" in order to transfer resources from private to public control and hence from consumption to investment.

The *Quarterly Journal of Economics* article just cited [*19*] derives shadow prices to replace both willingness to pay and the nominal value of public investment funds under a variety of assumptions about the shape of the consumption stream

[1] This analysis offers some rationalization of the policy of emphasizing heavy industry in the allocation of public investment funds, a policy followed in India and elsewhere on intuitive grounds.

generated by private investment and reinvestment. (The assumptions of the present discussion are chosen as much for expositional simplicity as for correspondence to reality.) In addition to examining the implications of alternative assumptions about displacement and reinvestment, the article shows how the difference between "shadow" and private willingness to pay for outputs can be reflected in the shadow price of public investment funds, thus enabling planners to measure aggregate consumption benefits by willingness to pay regardless of the use to which outputs are put. The formula for the shadow price, or cutoff benefit-cost ratio, that permits this to be done is

$$a = \frac{\theta\rho + (1 - \theta)\,\bar{r}}{\mu\rho + (1 - \mu)\,\bar{r}}\,. \tag{2.5}$$

Note that a nonzero reinvestment coefficient μ reduces the value of the shadow price (2.5) below the value of the shadow price (2.4), which reflects only displacement. Moreover, the value of (2.5) is less than unity if the reinvestment coefficient μ is greater than the displacement coefficient θ.

Under certain circumstances we can even further simplify reflection in the intertemporal criterion of the social rate of discount, displacement of private investment, and reinvestment. If public sector projects can be classified into groups in such a manner that within each group

1. the displacement (θ) and reinvestment (μ) coefficients, as well as the rate of return on displaced investment and reinvestment (ρ), are the same for all projects,
2. the economic lives of all projects are the same,

   and if, moreover, it can be assumed for planning purposes that
3. the benefit rates of all projects are constant until the termination of their economic lives,[1]

then the effects on project design of displacement, reinvestment, and the social rate of discount can be combined in a single "synthetic" rate of discount for use in conjunction with a cutoff benefit-cost ratio of unity. The synthetic discount rate defines the minimum rate of return that project increments in each group must earn in order to qualify for inclusion in the

[1] In consequence of a rule derived later in this chapter under the heading "Dynamics," this assumption is less restrictive than it might appear.

public sector programme under the aggregate consumption objective.

The method of computing this synthetic rate of discount—or, rather, set of rates because the synthetic rate will vary from group to group—is straightforward. For the group of projects with economic lives of T years, the objective function

$$\sum_{t=1}^{T} \frac{B_t(x)}{(1+\bar{r})^t} - aK(x) \tag{2.3}$$

is equal, by virtue of the constancy of benefits, to

$$\frac{1-(1+r)^{-T}}{\bar{r}} B_t(x) - aK(x). \tag{2.6}$$

Since multiplication of each term of the objective function by the same number does not alter project design, maximization of time-weighted aggregate consumption benefits, as in expressions (2.1) and (2.6), is equivalent to maximization of

$$\frac{1}{a} \times \frac{1-(1+\bar{r})^{-T}}{\bar{r}} B_t(x) - K(x). \tag{2.7}$$

The synthetic discount rate s is thus the discount rate that solves the following equation:

$$\frac{1-(1+s)^{-T}}{s} = \frac{1}{a} \times \frac{1-(1+\bar{r})^{-T}}{\bar{r}} \tag{2.8}$$

In other words, with s defined by equation (2.8) the objective function

$$\sum_{t=1}^{T} \frac{B_t(x)}{(1+s)^t} - K(x). \tag{2.9}$$

is equivalent to the objective function (2.3).

For simplicity let us suppose that ρ, θ, and μ are the same not only for all projects within a single group but for all groups. Then with the assumption of constant benefit streams, projects can be classified according to longevity alone. Hence s can be calculated directly from T by means of equation (2.8). Table 2.1 gives hypothetical values of the synthetic discount rate to be used together with a shadow price of unity in place of the social rate of discount $\bar{r}$ together with the shadow price a.

It is assumed that $\bar{r} = 0{\cdot}05$, $\rho = 0{\cdot}10$, $\theta = 0{\cdot}90$, and $\mu = 0{\cdot}50$, with the result that

$$a = \frac{\theta\rho + (1 - \theta)\,\bar{r}}{\mu\rho + (1 - \mu)\,\bar{r}} = 1{\cdot}265. \tag{2.10}$$

TABLE 2.1

Synthetic Discount Rate as function of Social Rate of Discount, Shadow Price,† and Economic Life*

Economic Life of Public Sector Projects (Years) T	Approximate Synthetic Discount Rate s
10	0·12
20	0·08
50	0·0665
∞	0·0635

* $\bar{r} = 0{\cdot}05$. † $a = 1{\cdot}265$.

Thus, paradoxically, the rule that public sector investment must provide the same marginal value of aggregate consumption as alternative private uses of resources, both evaluated at the social rate of discount, requires that the cutoff (marginal) rate of return for public investment projects vary inversely with the project's economic life.[1]

This is a good point at which to examine the *practical* consequences for public investment of reflecting private investment opportunities as I have suggested—by means of a shadow price of capital coupled with a social rate of discount or a synthetic rate of discount—instead of reflecting private opportunities by the more conventional method of discounting public investment returns at ρ (or r^*). My "social-rate-cum-opportunity-cost" criterion differs from the conventional criterion in its effects on both the size and the composition of public investment.

[1] If $\bar{r}$ exceeds ρ, then s will vary directly with T. In view of the current debate in socialist countries as to whether or not the marginal rate of return should differ among branches of investment, the dependence of s on T (and other parameters) is of theoretical as well as practical significance.

If ρ exceeds $\bar{r}$, then the "social-rate-cum-opportunity-cost" criterion generally imposes a less stringent test on potential public projects because it places a lower value on the portion of investment costs that come from private consumption or from "slack" than on the portion that comes from private investment, whereas the conventional criterion implicitly assumes that all resources for public investment come out of private investment. The "social-rate-cum-opportunity-cost" criterion is made even less stringent if, as in (2.5), it allows for reinvestment of the benefits from public projects. Thus a public investment programme formulated according to this criterion can be expected to be larger than one formulated according to its more conventional rival.[1]

The difference between the two criteria with respect to the volume of public investment is less important in a planned economy, however, than in an unplanned economy—if the planned economy determines the over-all size of public investment and its division among competing branches by means of

[1] This conclusion is stated somewhat tentatively because the difference between my criterion and the conventional one with respect to the size of public investment depends, first, on the longevity of public investment and, second, on the values of θ and μ. The importance of the economic life of public projects can be appreciated by comparing the operation of the synthetic discount rate form of my criterion with the operation of the conventional one. For simplicity, suppose for the moment that all public projects have constant benefit rates over their economic life. Then, with the assumed values of the parameters of a in Table 2.1, the "social-rate-cum-opportunity-cost" criterion imposes a cutoff rate of return of 12 per cent if all public projects have an economic life of 10 years; therefore my criterion would reject investments that would qualify if they had to show a rate of return equal only to ρ, namely, 10 per cent. On the other hand, if all public projects have an economic life of 20 years (or more), then my criterion imposes a cutoff rate of return of only 8 per cent (or less) and thus provides a less stringent test than a ρ of 10 per cent.

The effect of the values of θ and μ can be seen by considering the extreme case of $\theta = 1$ and $\mu = 0$. In this case the synthetic rate of discount is higher than ρ for all values of T (T measures economic life) less than infinity; because the relevant private opportunity is assumed to be a perpetuity, the private opportunity has a higher present value at the social rate of discount than any public opportunity with the same internal rate of return but a finite life. Hence in this extreme case my criterion would lead to a public investment programme certainly no larger, and possibly smaller, than the conventional criterion would produce.

budgetary constraints (see pp. 69–71). Given the present state of the planning art, budgetary constraints framed in accordance with quinquennial and annual plans can at best reflect the rate of discount only very imperfectly, and it is difficult to imagine that planning techniques will improve sufficiently rapidly to allow the rate of discount to play an explicit role in determining the quantitative shape of plans within the near future.

Thus it is the difference in its effect on the composition of investment programmes, that is, on the choice among competing projects, that in the Indian context is most important in distinguishing my criterion from its more conventional rival. If economic merit is judged in terms of the social rate of discount, direct use of ρ as a discount rate introduces undue discrimination against capital-intensive or durable projects as a consequence of trying to ensure that public investment is at least as meritorious as the alternative private economic activity. Evaluation of the present value of benefits at the discount rate $\bar{r}$ and of capital costs at a rupees per rupee introduces no such bias in accomplishing the same goal of equalizing the marginal effectiveness of all kinds of investment.

The discrimination introduced by requiring all public investment, whatever its economic life, to earn the same marginal rate of return (ρ) emerges clearly from contrasting the constant rate of return imposed by the conventional criterion with the variable cutoff marginal rate of return embodied in the synthetic rate of discount. The variable synthetic rate of discount incorporates both $\bar{r}$ and a and equalizes the marginal effectiveness of projects of different longevities—effectiveness judged, naturally, in terms of the social rate of discount. Questions of capital intensity and longevity become important in choosing between, say, short-lived but capital-saving tube wells and long-lived but capital-intensive surface reservoirs in the formulation of an irrigation programme.

The differences between the "social-rate-cum-opportunity-cost" criterion and the conventional criterion with respect to both the size and the composition of public investment can be illustrated graphically. Suppose, for example, that two projects, A and B, each entail unit capital costs and that their relative aggregate consumption streams are as depicted in Figure 2.3.

In this simple case no sophisticated rule is required to choose *A* over *B*. *A* has a higher present value than *B* regardless of the interest rate at which the two streams are evaluated, as shown in Figure 2.4. Thus, whether we compare the differences

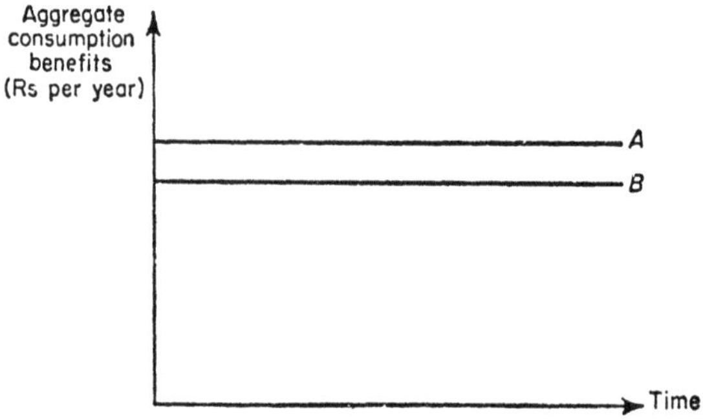

Figure 2.3. Nonintersecting aggregate consumption streams of two hypothetical projects

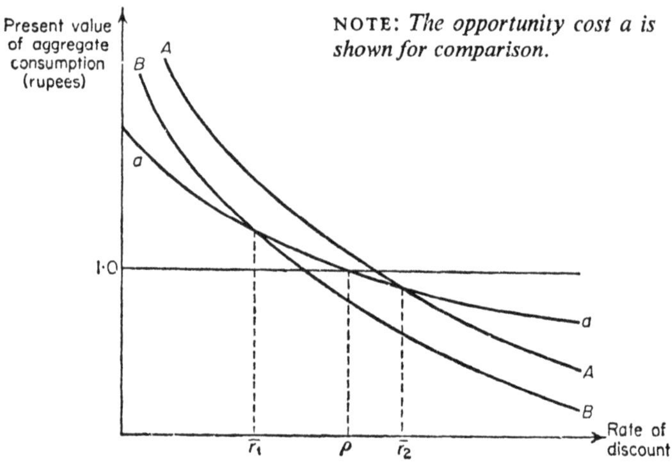

Figure 2.4. Present values of aggregate consumption streams shown in Figure 2.3 as functions of the rate of discount

between present values of benefits at the discount rate ρ and evaluate capital costs at the nominal price of Re 1·00 per rupee or we compare the differences between present values of benefits at a social rate of discount (like $\bar{r}_1$) and evaluate capital costs at the shadow price a, we come to the same conclusion: Choose A in preference to B.

But even in this simple case the choice of the intertemporal criterion affects the size of public investment. Direct use of ρ as a discount rate leads to acceptance only of A; B's present value evaluated at the discount rate ρ is less than its capital costs. Similarly, evaluation of time streams at any social rate of discount between $\bar{r}_1$ and $\bar{r}_2$ gives A, but not B, a present value in excess of the cost of capital measured in terms of the shadow price a. On the other hand, social rates of discount less than $\bar{r}_1$ give both A and B present values in excess of opportunity costs and hence lead to acceptance of both.

The criterion becomes even more important when the time streams of different projects intersect, as do the consumption streams of C and D in Figure 2.5, or in the special case of

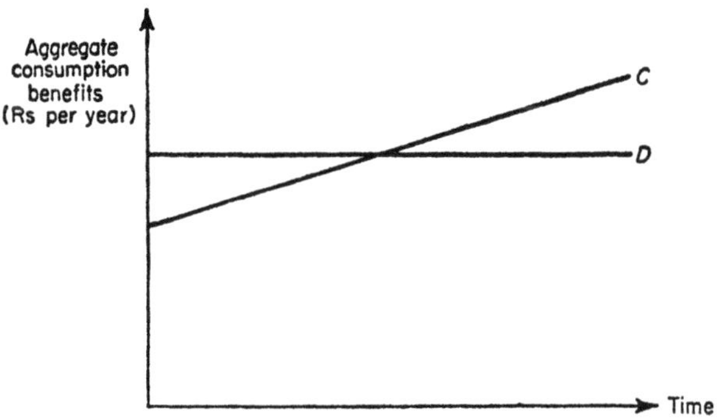

Figure 2.5. Intersecting consumption streams of two hypothetical projects

intersecting time streams that occurs when projects have different economic lives, as depicted in Figure 2.6. In both cases, functions relating present values to the discount rate will characteristically have the shape of Figure 2.7. D has the greater present value at all discount rates higher than the "break-even rate" $\bar{r}_0$, and C has the greater present value at discount rates lower than $\bar{r}_0$. Here the possibility arises that the two criteria will lead to conflicting rankings, and this is indeed the situation illustrated in Figure 2.7. Comparison of present values of benefits at the discount rate ρ, or at any discount rate in excess of $\bar{r}_0$, leads to the conclusion that D is superior to C, but comparison of present values at any social rate of discount lower than $\bar{r}_0$ leads to a preference for C over D.

Moreover, social discount rates lower than $\bar{r}_1$ give both C and

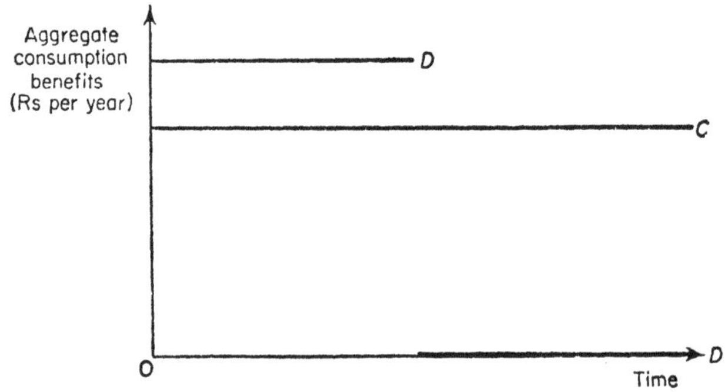

Figure 2.6. Consumption streams of projects of different economic lives

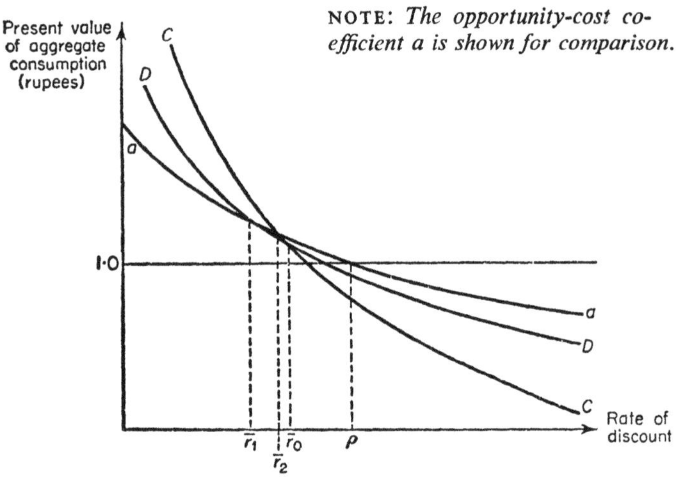

NOTE: *The opportunity-cost coefficient a is shown for comparison.*

Figure 2.7. Present values of aggregate consumption streams in Figures 2.5 and 2.6 as functions of the discount rate

D a present value of aggregate consumption benefits in excess of capital costs evaluated at the shadow price a. Social rates between $\bar{r}_1$ and $\bar{r}_2$ imply that the present value of C's benefits exceed the opportunity cost of capital and that the present value of D's benefits do not. At higher interest rates neither C nor D passes the test imposed by my criterion. Nor does either project qualify under the conventional criterion, since the present value of benefits of both projects at the discount rate ρ is less than the nominal capital cost.

Intertemporal criteria for objectives other than aggregate consumption. The principles governing intertemporal criteria are the same for all objectives. The rate of discount measures the percentage rate at which the relative weight on contributions to the objective decreases over time.[1] The calculation of the shadow price of investment costs proceeds along the same lines that led to equation (2.4). The investment-displacement coefficient θ is defined for other objectives as for the aggregate consumption objective, that is, as the amount of private investment each rupee of public investment displaces. The parameter ρ represents the annual contribution of private investment to the objective in question, and the coefficient θ^* represents the present sacrifice that public investment would entail with respect to the objective. These definitions simply represent generalizations of the definition of θ, ρ, and θ^* *vis-à-vis* the aggregate consumption objective.[2] Although important reinvestment effects undoubtedly exist with respect to all objectives, it is not expedient to attempt to reflect reinvestment indirectly in the shadow price for objectives other than aggregate consumption.[3] The opportunity cost for other objectives is therefore

$$a = \theta \frac{\rho}{r} + \theta^*, \qquad (2.11)$$

where r is the rate of discount for the objective in question.[4]

[1] It would therefore be pure coincidence if the discount rates for two or more objectives were equal.

[2] For objectives other than aggregate consumption even less than for the aggregate consumption objective is it to be expected that θ and θ^* add up to unity, that is, θ^* in general is not equal to $(1 - \theta)$ as in equation (2.4).

[3] Indirect reflection of reinvestment is infeasible because, for objectives other than aggregate consumption, there is no constant μ by which willingness to pay can be multiplied to calculate even the approximate effects of reinvestment on benefits. Hence the additional contribution to these objectives from reinvestment must be measured directly.

[4] A synthetic discount rate for use with a shadow price of unity can be computed, but the limitations on the use of this device imposed by the homogeneity assumptions listed on p. 59 also apply here.

Further discussion of time and interest criteria requires examination of each objective separately. Specifically, let us consider briefly—by way of illustration—the choice of a discount rate for the self-sufficiency objective. If for the sake of definiteness we equate self-sufficiency with its first meaning, balance of trade, then the self-sufficiency discount rate (which will be denoted r_s) places contributions to the balance of payments that occur at different times on a common footing with present contributions to this objective. Thus the total benefits to a hypothetical objective function reflecting contributions to aggregate consumption and national self-sufficiency are

$$\left\{\sum_{t=1}^{\infty} \frac{B_t(x)}{(1+\bar{r})^t} - aK(x)\right\} + w_s\left\{\sum_{t=1}^{\infty} \frac{S_t(x)}{(1+{}_s\bar{r})^t} - a_sK_s(x)\right\}.$$

The terms in braces to the left of the plus sign represent aggregate consumption benefits as defined in expression (2.3). The terms on the right within braces reflect self-sufficiency benefits and costs: $S_t(x)$ gives self-sufficiency benefits net of self-sufficiency costs in year t from a project (or programme) of scale x; a_s, as defined in expression (2.11), is the opportunity cost in terms of foreign exchange earnings foregone in the private sector for each rupee of present foreign exchange devoted to public investment; $K_s(x)$ reflects the direct and indirect (see the section headed "Secondary Benefits" in this chapter) foreign exchange component of capital costs. The number by which the net self-sufficiency benefits are multiplied, w_s, represents the weight placed on present contributions to self-sufficiency relative to contributions to aggregate consumption.

The parameter w_s is the shadow price of foreign exchange expressed as a percentage of the official exchange rate; it represents the marginal value in terms of present aggregate consumption of a rupee's worth of current imports. Since exports and imports are reflected only in the self-sufficiency objective (not in the aggregate consumption objective) this definition of w_s does not represent double-counting.[1] $w_s/(1+r_s)^t$ is the price of foreign exchange earnings in year t relative to

[1] A lower limit to w_s is given by the marginal consumption value a rupee's worth of imports would have if all aid obtainable now and in the future were utilized—so that self-sufficiency were completely sacrificed for the sake of other goals.

present consumption; in other words, the self-sufficiency rate of discount r_s reflects the rate at which the price of foreign exchange relative to present consumption declines with time. If the relative importance of *future* contributions to self-sufficiency and aggregate consumption is expected to remain the same as the relative importance of present contributions to the two objectives, then the self-sufficiency rate of discount r_s is equal to the aggregate consumption rate of discount $\bar{r}$. r_s is greater than $\bar{r}$ if the importance of self-sufficiency relative to aggregate consumption decreases over time, and r_s is smaller than $\bar{r}$ if the relative importance of self-sufficiency increases over time.

It may be thought that actual interest rates on external debt can guide policymakers in the choice of a self-sufficiency discount rate. Unfortunately, interest rates on loans from abroad are no more relevant to the choice of a self-sufficiency discount rate than are market interest rates to the choice of an interest rate for aggregate consumption.

To see why merely requires examination of the decision whether or not to accept, say, a 6% twenty-year loan of Rs 1 crore to be repaid in equal annual instalments. In principle policymakers ought to accept the loan if and only if the weighted sum of net contributions made possible by the loan to all objectives is positive, with the annual repayment of Rs 872 lakhs[1] included as a cost in calculating self-sufficiency benefits. That is to say, loans are properly accepted or rejected on the basis of their contributions to all objectives, not just self-sufficiency, so the acceptance-rejection decision does not tell us anything about the rate at which the value of contributions to self-sufficiency declines over time, and it is this rate of decline that r_s measures. Actual rates of interest on external debt would reflect policymakers' intertemporal preferences with respect to self-sufficiency only if the sole effect of foreign borrowing was to decrease future reliance on aid.

Budgetary Constraints

It was suggested in the previous section that the opportunity cost of public investment falls to the extent that public investment can mobilize unemployed resources. In essence, mobiliza-

[1] 1 lakh = 100 thousand. Rs 872 lakhs is the annual payment required to repay a loan of Rs 1 crore in twenty equal annual instalments when 6% interest is charged on the outstanding balance.

tion of unemployed resources means more labour-intensive use of existing capital goods in public construction. The problem is that workers engaged in public investment must be paid a positive wage; *corvée* is not politically feasible in Indian conditions. Expansion of public expenditure through deficit financing would cause inflation, and expansion through taxation would directly reduce disposable money income for some segments of the population. Since either method would cause real disposable income to fall for some groups, political limitations exist to the mobilization of unemployed labour for the expansion of labour-intensive investment.[1]

An effective limitation on the financial resources available to the public sector should be reflected in project plans through the shadow price of capital. In such a situation of "capital rationing," this shadow price represents an *internal* opportunity cost to the public sector, namely, the marginal present value of public investment outlay at the social rate of discount.[2] If we evaluate private utilization of resources only from the point of view of the contribution to aggregate consumption, the value per rupee of budgetary "slack" is a; that is, the aggregate consumption value per rupee of unused portions of the public sector capital budget is the *external* shadow price of investment funds with respect to the aggregate consumption objective. The internal shadow price falls to a, and a becomes relevant, only if the budgetary constraint turns out to be non-binding. Thus a consequence of a binding budgetary constraint is to prevent the government from carrying public investment to the point at which its marginal effectiveness falls to the level

[1] The problem of resource mobilization posed by the conflict between the interest of the employed and the interest of the unemployed is apparently not limited to mixed-enterprise economies like India. Joseph Pajestka describes the same problem in the Polish context in Oskar Lange, ed. [*15*], especially pp. 320–324, and in the International Labour Office report on employment and development [*14*], pp. 199–208.

[2] An internal shadow price can, like an external one, be combined with the social rate of discount to form a set of synthetic rates of discount; the design rule for aggregate consumption maximization can then be stated as equality of each project's marginal rate of return with the appropriate synthetic rate of discount. This rule should be contrasted with the conventional rule for situations of financial scarcity, namely, maximization of the internal rate of return on the available funds.

of the marginal effectiveness in increasing aggregate consumption of private resource utilization.

Besides the general limitation on financial resources, specific budgetary constraints may be placed on various branches of public investment as a means of implementing the strategic decisions of the five-year plans. These budgetary subconstraints ensure at least approximate adherence to the planned composition of the growth of public sector output, and reduce to manageable proportions the range of alternatives to be subjected to benefit-cost analysis. Differences in the internal shadow prices of capital among branches would indicate differences in the marginal effectiveness of investment and would suggest the desirability of at least marginal transfers of resources from the branches in which the marginal effectiveness is low to those in which it is high.

Risk and Uncertainty

By definition, present investment yields its returns only as the future unfolds, and the results of all investment are therefore inherently uncertain. Since public sector projects tend typically to be more durable than private projects, uncertainty is consequently all the more important in the economic analysis of public investment.

We can distinguish between two kinds of uncertainty: risk, and uncertainty proper. A *risky* situation is one in which the probability distribution of outcomes is known; an *uncertain* situation is one in which even this information is totally lacking. The fact that the world invariably presents situations that lie between the two extremes does not render the dichotomy useless, any more than the dichotomy between monopoly and competition is useless because the characteristics of industry fall between the assumptions of these two models.

Let us consider risk first. Examples of situations that lie close to this end of the spectrum are provided by doubts about the outcome of investments that stem from vagaries of weather, for example, the doubts about irrigation projects that arise from lack of precise knowledge about precipitation. We cannot predict next year's runoff of the Sutlej River accurately, but on the basis of past performance we can with confidence assign probabilities to various levels of runoff and available water. The problem of how to employ the parameters of probability distributions describing risky situations in the design and operation of investment projects has received extensive attention in the literature of economic theory, although the theory is as yet incomplete and inconclusive.[1]

The main point for present purposes is that the existence of risk requires policymakers to specify their attitudes toward risk. Specification might be explicit, for example, in terms of the rate at which they are willing to trade greater average returns for less variance or skewness in returns; or specification might be implicit in terms of constraints on variance and skewness. It is to be emphasized that one's attitude towards variance and skewness in the output of an individual project depends upon the objective. From the point of view of aggregate consumption the fluctuations in output from many independent projects may very nearly cancel each other out every year. This may be small consolation, however, with respect to the objective of raising consumption in a particular group or region dependent on a particular project—at least in the absence of an insurance scheme for reproducing for each group and region the reductions of variance and skewness attained by aggregation.

The uncertainty inherent in projections of benefits and costs presents a more formidable problem precisely because our knowledge is based only on hunch and insight. The effects of technological change, changes in tastes, deviations from planned levels of investment, and changes in international conditions on investment benefits can at best be seen "through a glass, darkly," and to attempt to analyse these sources of uncertainty in terms of probability distributions appropriate to risky situations is at best premature.

This statement is not meant as an endorsement of conventional techniques for handling uncertainty. The three approaches suggested by the *Green Book* [*28*], pp. 22–23, are typical of the conventional wisdom and are generally inappropriate for public

[1] Two excellent accounts of risk and uncertainty that are especially relevant for public sector decisions are given in Arthur Maass and others [*16*], pp. 129–158, and Pierre Massé [*21*], Chapters 5–8. Details of application of the theory of risk to the design of water-resources systems appear on pp. 273–278 and in Chapters 12 and 14 of [*16*].

investment decisions. First, the *Green Book* recommends conservatism in estimating benefits and costs. Benefit estimates are to be reduced and cost estimates increased in rough proportion to the analyst's lack of confidence in the expected values. The aversion to uncertainty implied by such a criterion reflects a pessimism that is not, and ought not to be, necessarily the attitude of the government.[1] This is especially true in the analysis of independent projects in relation to aggregative objectives. The below par performance or even failure of some projects may be balanced by an unexpected degree of success on the part of others. The fact that the nonactuarial nature of uncertainty makes an insurance scheme impractical does not vitiate the "safety in numbers" that a group of independent projects offers *vis-à-vis* aggregation objectives such as aggregate consumption and self-sufficiency.[2]

The second suggestion of the *Green Book* is the addition of a premium to the discount rate that, like the penalty assigned to benefits and costs, varies directly with the lack of confidence in benefit and cost estimates. The basic objection to this device is the same as the objection to doctoring benefit and cost estimates—that it represents what might be an inordinate aversion to uncertainty. The only circumstances in which the addition of an uncertainty premium to the discount rate would seem justified are those in which it is thought necessary to reflect the possibility of total failure of a project, under the assumption that the probabilities of failure in different time intervals are independent of one other.[3]

[1] Both Alan Manne and Amartya Sen have suggested that, though conservatism in benefit and cost estimates may not be an appropriate means of counteracting uncertainty in "expected values," conservatism is an appropriate countermeasure for the invariably optimistic bias of the technicians who estimate benefits and costs. The problem of devising measures to keep planners "honest" is beyond the scope of the present discussion, whatever the biases of technicians.

[2] In fact, safety in numbers is a powerful argument for the public as opposed to private undertaking of uncertain ventures. And even where doubts are of the risky rather than the uncertain variety, and therefore insurable at least in principle, public enterprise may be preferred to private on the grounds that the "self-insurance" open to the public sector is less costly than the establishment of companies to provide insurance.

[3] Or we might interpret the assumption of independence of probabilities over time as reflecting the possibility of total annihilation of the world.

The third suggestion of the *Green Book* is conservative estimation of the economic life of projects. Once again there is comparatively little justification for this procedure in any situation, especially in situations where a large number of independent projects contribute to aggregative objectives.

Thus the basic points, which are valid for both risk and uncertainty, are, first, that policymakers must specify their attitudes towards fluctuations in benefits and costs rather than abdicate this value judgment to subordinates who introduce their own biases under the guise of technical criteria akin to the safety criteria for loading bridges. Second, the public sector should take advantage of the facility that the size and variety of public sector investments offer for pooling risks and uncertainties, a facility that allows a greater tolerance of variance and skewness in the performance of individual projects by public decision-makers than by private decision-makers, even supposing equal aversion to fluctuations in the performance of entire programmes.

Additional counsel on uncertainty is left to the next section, which treats specifically of the dynamics of investment planning.

Dynamics

This section briefly investigates the "when" of investment decisions, the optimal timing of projects in view of changes in the benefit rates of projects over time. In a sense the problem arises from the explicit form of the criterion introduced earlier for intertemporal comparisons, namely, the present value of net benefits. Although superior to alternative criteria like maximization of the rate of return in the public sector, or minimization of the "pay-out period,"[1] naïve use of the present-value criterion can lead to more severe errors *vis-à-vis* the dynamic question of construction times for projects than do otherwise inferior criteria.

A numerical example will serve to illustrate the pitfalls

[1] A project's pay-out period is defined as the number of years the project requires for its benefits net of operating costs to equal its capital costs. The pay-out period is a popular test of the worthiness of proposed investments in American business practice, but Alan Manne's impression, conveyed verbally, is that this criterion is gradually giving way to the criterion of present value.

inherent in naïve application of the present-value criterion. Suppose we are asked to analyse a proposal for the construction of an irrigation project, and for definiteness let us suppose the sole objective is maximization of the contribution of the project to aggregate consumption. Let us suppose further that agricultural production per acre-foot of irrigation water is expected to increase over time as a result of development of higher yielding varieties of crops, greater use of fertilizers and plant protection measures by a more educated and aware peasantry, and other improved techniques. For simplicity of calculation we shall reflect the increase in value in the form of a single step in the benefit function: Starting with a hypothetical present, 1970, we shall suppose that the potential annual benefit from the project, net of operating costs, is Rs 1 crore from 1971 through 1990 and Rs 10 crores annually from 1991 forward. In this example we assume that the increase in benefits is independent of project age. That is, we ignore any influence of the project on varietal improvement, education and awareness of peasants, and so forth, and we assume full utilization of irrigation facilities in the year following construction. (The benefit in 1995, for example, will be Rs 10 crores whether the project is then one or twenty years old.) Next we suppose that the capital cost of the project is Rs 100 crores regardless of the year in which construction is undertaken. Finally, we assume the social rate of discount to be 5 per cent and, for simplicity, the shadow price of capital to be unity.

Now we are ready to proceed. If constructed in 1970, the present value of the project's benefits, net of operating costs but not net of capital costs, is Rs 87·84 crores.[1] Since the project's

[1] The computations:

(*a*) The present value of the benefits from 1971 to 1991 is derived from the formula for the present value of a twenty-year annuity of Rs 1 crore:

$$1 \times 0{\cdot}05^{-1} \times (1 - 1{\cdot}05^{-20}) = \text{Rs } 12{\cdot}462 \text{ crores.}$$

(*b*) The present value of the benefits from 1991 forward is obtained by calculating the present value of a perpetuity of Rs 10 crores beginning twenty years hence:

$$10 \times 0{\cdot}05^{-1} \times 1{\cdot}05^{-20} = \text{Rs } 75{\cdot}378 \text{ crores.}$$

(*c*) The present value of total benefits is the sum of the results in (*a*) and (*b*):

$$12{\cdot}462 + 75{\cdot}378 = \text{Rs } 87{\cdot}840 \text{ crores.}$$

capital cost is Rs 100 crores, its 1970 present value for immediate construction is negative: —Rs 12·16 crores. As prudent investors we must clearly reject present construction of the project.

But what about construction of the project in future years? Let us look at the cost side first. The 1970 present value of capital cost for construction in year u (counting 1970 as year zero) is Rs 100 crores $\times$ $1{\cdot}05^{-u}$. Similarly the present value of construction in year $u + 1$ is Rs 100 crores $\times$ $1{\cdot}05^{-(u+1)}$. The difference between the 1970 present value of the cost of construction in year u and $u + 1$ is

$$100 \times 1{\cdot}05^{-u} - 100 \times 1{\cdot}05^{-(u+1)} \tag{2.12}$$

Simplifying expression (2.12), it becomes

$$100 \times 0{\cdot}05 \times 1{\cdot}05^{-(u+1)} = 5 \times 1{\cdot}05^{-(u+1)}. \tag{2.13}$$

Rs 5 crores is the annual interest cost of Rs 100 crores at 5 per cent; it is the social value of postponing a sacrifice of Rs 100 crores of consumption for one year. Multiplication by $1{\cdot}05^{-(u+1)}$ converts the interest cost to its present value.

On the benefit side, postponement of construction from year u to year $u + 1$ results simply in the loss of the u + 1st year's benefits; the loss in 1970 present value of benefits caused by a year's postponement is thus

$1 \times 1{\cdot}05^{-(u+1)}$ $u = 0, \ldots, 19$ (that is, from 1970 through 1989, (2.14a)

$10 \times 1{\cdot}05^{-(u+1)}$ $u = 20, \ldots,$ (that is, from 1990 forward). (2.14b)

The change in *net* present value resulting from postponement of construction by a year is the difference between the saving in interest cost and the loss in benefits, that is, the difference between the value of expression (2.13) and the value of expression (2.14):

$$(5 - 1 = 4) \times 1{\cdot}05^{-(u+1)} \quad u = 0, \ldots, 19 \tag{2.15a}$$

$$(5 - 10 = -5) \times 1{\cdot}05^{-(u+1)} \quad u = 20, \ldots \tag{2.15b}$$

From expression (2.15a) we see that until 1989 the change in net present value from delaying construction is positive; the annual saving in interest cost of Rs 5 crores exceeds the annual loss of benefits of Rs 1 crore. Thus until 1989 the 1970 net present value of the project increases with each year that construction is postponed. In 1990, however, because of the increase in the benefit rate, the marginal net present value of postponing construction changes sign. After 1990 the annual benefit exceeds the annual interest cost, and, as expression (2.15b) indicates, 1970 net present value decreases with each year that construction is postponed beyond 1990. The maximum net present value is thus obtained by constructing the project in 1990, and the project has quite a handsome payoff for 1990 construction: a 1970 net present value of Rs 37·689 crores and an over-all benefit cost ratio of 2:1.[1]

The relationship of 1970 net present value to the time of construction is shown graphically in Figure 2.8. One fact is worthy of special note. Reliance upon a static "to build or not to build" analysis for 1970 construction alone would lead us, correctly, to reject the irrigation project because of its negative net present value for present construction, but a similar analysis in 1975 would lead us, incorrectly as it turns out, to construct the project then. The present value of the project increases for more than fifteen years after the project is first "justified," that is, for more than fifteen years after construction first yields a positive net present value.

The starkness of these results admittedly is in part due to the simplifying assumptions I have made. Nevertheless, the lessons have general validity. The problem of dynamic criteria is explored in more detail and with assumptions more closely attuned to the world in an article by Alan Manne [*17*] and in a monograph of my own [*18*]. Kenneth Arrow [2] has generalized the discussion in a more abstract framework. For the present I shall simply state one criterion that can be applied in a fairly wide variety of cases. If

[1] The computations:

(*a*) As shown in the preceding note, the 1970 present value of benefits from 1991 forward is Rs 75·378 crores.

(*b*) The 1970 present value of capital costs for 1990 construction is Rs 37·689 crores.

(*c*) The 1970 net present value is the difference between these two figures, and their ratio is the benefit-cost ratio.

1. the costs of indivisible projects or increments are independent,
2. marginal benefits do not increase with the scale of the project but do increase over time,
3. gestation periods can be ignored, and
4. the shadow price of capital reflects the appropriate external or internal opportunity cost,

then optimal scheduling results can be achieved by scheduling each project or increment for construction the first time the project shows a positive present value, *with the present value of benefits always computed on the (incorrect) assumption that the then current benefit rate will continue indefinitely*. This myopic rule incidentally allows us to escape a major kind of uncertainty,

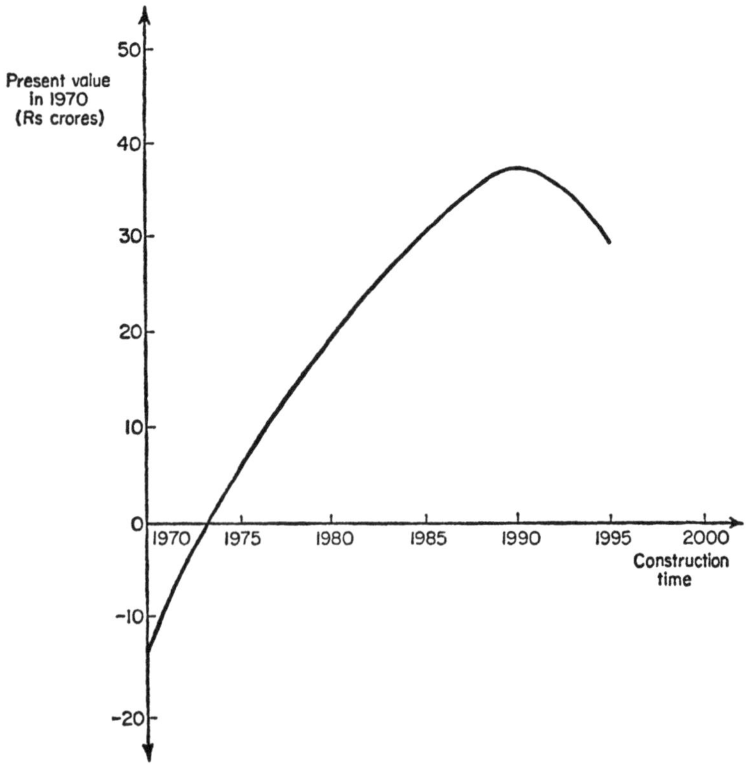

Figure 2.8. Net present value of a hypothetical irrigation project as a function of its construction time

namely, uncertainty as to future benefit rates. As long as we know that benefit rates are increasing we need not know future benefit rates exactly, for we can determine the optimal construction time sequentially by means of current benefit rates alone.[1]

Secondary Benefits

In the US context the term "secondary benefits" has played a dual role in benefit-cost analysis. Secondary benefits have referred both to indirect contributions of public investment to aggregate consumption that are not reflected in the willingness to pay of users of project outputs and to the entire contribution to all objectives other than aggregate consumption. Much of the confusion about the role of secondary benefits stems from this duality of purpose, and an unambiguous definition is the first step to clarity.

Once the multiplicity of objectives is explicitly recognized, no purpose is served by distinguishing the contributions to different objectives as "primary" and "secondary." Thus the second of the two roles of secondary benefits in the United States is not relevant to Indian benefit-cost analysis. On the other hand, since aggregate consumption is not the only objective for which the direct contribution of projects to immediate users of outputs may differ from the total contribution, the first role is too limited for the Indian context. Hence in this discussion secondary benefits will be defined separately for each

[1] This rule is derived in Marglin [*18*], pp. 22–24 and has been generalized by Arrow [*2*] to include the case of interest rates that vary over time. Just as it is the current benefit rate alone that is relevant to this "build or postpone" decision, so is it the current interest rate that is relevant. Of the many assumptions required to derive it the rule stated in the text, perhaps the most limiting is the assumption of independence among the costs of projects or increments. Substantial economies of scale may lead us to build ahead of benefits, and optimal construction time is determined by balancing interest costs, loss of benefits, and economies of scale. This problem is explicitly analysed in Manne [*17*].

Even in the absence of economies of scale, the sequential rule given in the text must be supplemented in situations in which some action must be taken prior to construction of a project—in order to prevent preemption of a desirable site, to ensure the availability of transport facilities, and so forth. It must also be slightly modified to account for gestation periods and other effects of project age.

objective as indirect contributions to objectives not reflected in the direct consumption of goods and services produced by public enterprises.

The aggregate consumption objective. One discrepancy between willingness to pay for goods and services and the contribution to aggregate consumption has already been analysed in connection with reinvestment, and no more need be said about its measurement now. Apart from reinvestment, the principal sources of secondary benefits with respect to the aggregate consumption objective are (1) departures from competition in the further processing of goods and services produced by means of public project outputs, (2) changes in consumption sufficient to produce changes in the prices of consumer goods, (3) external economies associated with public projects, and (4) private investment induced by public projects. These four sources of indirect benefits will be considered in order.

Departures from competition lead to secondary benefits in the following way. Suppose a public sector irrigation project provides water for the production of sugar cane. Ordinarily, as indicated at the beginning of this chapter, the growers' willingness to pay for irrigation can be taken as a measure of the contribution of the water to aggregate consumption. However, to the extent that refiners earn monopoly profits on the processing of cane, the cultivators' willingness to pay does not fully reflect irrigation's contribution to aggregate consumption. Some of the aggregate consumption gain accrues to the refiners, which is reflected in the fact that monopolist refiners would, if put to the test, be willing to contribute financially to the irrigation system rather than forgo the extraordinary profits they enjoy on the extra cane that the irrigation system enables them to process. Thus the economic analysis of public sector projects must include the identification of monopoly and an estimate of monopoly profits in the various stages of production in which the outputs of public sector projects enter.[1] Whether or not the government takes steps to eliminate monopoly profits is a separate question whose answer depends on the weight attached to each objective of public policy.

[1] See the *Consultants' Report* [29], pp. 25–27, and Arthur Maass and others [*16*], p. 49, for a further discussion of this category of secondary benefits from the point of view of this study.

The next source of secondary benefits lies in the provision of additions to the supplies of consumption goods so large that relative prices are changed. Suppose the hypothetical irrigation project leads to an increase in the production of sugar cane sufficiently great to make the price of sugar to consumers fall. In this situation the growers' willingness to pay (plus monopoly profits to refineries, if any) fails to reflect the consumption gains of consumers due to lower prices. The general rule is that when public sector programmes change the prices of goods and services in later stages of production, the willingness to pay of project users must be supplemented by the "consumers' surplus"[1] enjoyed by consumers other than project users.[2]

The third category of secondary benefits, those arising from external economies, presents even more formidable measurement problems. An external economy exists when the provision of a good or service for an economic unit or group of units either makes provision of another good or service possible at a lower cost or makes provision of the same good or service to another unit or group of units possible at lower costs. (An external diseconomy results when the provision of a good or service necessarily provides a "bad" or a disservice.)

For an example of an externality we might return to our hypothetical irrigation scheme. Inevitably construction and maintenance of a canal system necessitate a system of access roads. Viewed as part of the irrigation scheme, the road system is simply one component of costs. However, it may also improve communications and lower transport costs for the villages served by the irrigation scheme. The additions to aggregate consumption provided by improved communications and lower transportation costs ought rightly to be included among the benefits of the irrigation scheme, even though they are simply by-products of the provision of water.

The formidable nature of the problem of measuring external economies, to which allusion has already been made, is a result of the lack of guide rules for identifying this type of secondary benefits. Many external economies—for example, the

[1] The consumers' surplus is the difference between the willingness to pay of the consumer and the competitive market value.

[2] The effect of price changes on aggregate consumption benefits is analysed in greater detail in Arthur Maass and others [*16*], pp. 55–58.

services of army engineers in the construction of bridges and dams in peacetime—cannot be measured with any acceptable degree of accuracy, and this should be recognized as a limitation of benefit-cost analysis. The alternative of claiming that a benefit-cost statement reflects *all* the consequences of public investment even with respect to so limited an objective as aggregate consumption would serve only to discredit benefit-cost analysis *in toto*.

The irrigation project can also serve to illustrate the fourth category of secondary benefits: induced investment. The availability of water (coupled with an effective agricultural extension service) can lead to the introduction of crops that cannot be grown under dry-farming conditions, and, *pari passu*, to investment by agriculturalists in fertilizers, plant protection, and conservation measures. To the extent that the private rate of discount exceeds the social rate, the social value of such induced investment will be greater than its value to the agriculturalist and therefore will not be adequately reflected in willingness to pay—even if the agriculturalist possesses full knowledge of the investment opportunities created by irrigation.

Redistribution objectives. Each class of secondary benefits discussed in connection with the aggregate consumption objective has its counterpart in redistribution objectives. The only qualification is the obvious one that the indirect benefits must accrue to the groups or regions selected for special attention under the redistribution goal. For example, with respect to the distribution of consumption between rich and poor, the consumers'-surplus effects of public investment that reduces the price of automobiles will differ from the effects of public investment that reduces the price of food grains even though the value of the consumers' surplus in terms of the aggregate consumption objectives may be identical in the two cases.

There are two additional and important sources of secondary benefits under the redistribution goal, especially in relation to a regional consumption objective. The entire value added to output by processing activities ancillary to a public project (with the exception of the portion of profits and wages remitted outside the region) represents a contribution to regional income, although only the supramarginal portion of value added represents a contribution to the aggregate consumption objective. Correspondingly the redistributional gains of projects ought to include the consumption afforded by the wages and profits from their construction and operation as well as from industries within the region that supply inputs to public enterprises. Of course, to list these gains under the aggregate consumption would clearly be double-counting.[1]

The other additional source of secondary benefits *vis-à-vis* a regional objective is the consumption produced by the spending of the beneficiaries of public projects and ancillary activities. As irrigation—to return once again to our earlier example—increases the incomes of cultivators, they consume more, and their expenditures give rise to additional employment, income, and consumption. The consumption of those who earn wages and profits from the sale of goods and services to the cultivators creates still more employment, income, and consumption, and so on in a chain reaction that fortunately need not be analysed step by step. The total effect of this chain reaction can be summarized by the "multiplier" analysis that has become a standard tool of economic theory. If we denote the cultivators' additional gross income (willingness to pay) from irrigation in a given year by W and their actual payments for irrigation by R, the direct contribution to a regional consumption objective is $(W - R)$. If we next denote the proportion of additional production marketed by cultivators by the symbol m, their additional cash income is $m(W - R)$. Assuming the marginal propensity to spend income on consumer goods and services within the region is the same for all inhabitants of the region and denoting its numerical value by e—the marginal "leakage," including savings and imports from outside the region, is $(1 - e)$—the secondary income generated within the region is

$$\frac{e}{1 - e} m(W - R).$$

[1] In theory a group redistributional objective requires a similar analysis of the effects of the growth of processing and supplying activities ancillary to public enterprises on the consumption generated to members of groups, rather than regions, designated by policymakers. Operationally, however, such an analysis is necessary only in the presence of some indication that the ancillary activities contribute more to the group redistribution objective than the activities displaced elsewhere in the economy.

If c is the marginal propensity to consume out of income, then the secondary consumption generated within the region is

$$\frac{e}{1-e}\,cm\,(W-R).$$

A similar multiplier process is set in motion by the spending of the wage component of construction and operating costs of the irrigation project as well as by the spending of wages and profits from ancillary processing and supplying industries created within the region. In fact many public projects create redistributional benefits *only* by means of the factor incomes that derive from construction and operation. Any project which provides only a small increment to the total supply of a particular good or service sold in a competitive market redistributes no income from differences between willingness to pay and actual charges, for in these circumstances willingness to pay for the project's output and actual charges are necessarily equal. A textile factory producing for a national market is a case in point; unlike our hypothetical irrigation project, the typical textile mill is generally too small to bring about a difference between W and R within the producing region.

The multiplier chain is of course not relevant to the aggregate consumption objective, since it represents no gain for the economy as a whole unless the obstacle to expansion of consumption is under-utilization of productive capacity because of inadequate demand.[1]

Merit-want objectives. It is difficult to imagine any class of secondary benefits other than external economies being important relative to the fulfilment of merit wants. An example of an external economy in the context of merit wants is the contribution of the defence establishment to national integration. The armed forces certainly do not exist to promote this particular goal but in many countries have contributed to *unum e pluribus*. More to the point, public investment in developing the transportation and communication network of the nation may make a large contribution to the goal of national integration. Un-

[1] A multiplier analysis should take place for a group redistribution objective in the event that the contribution of the chain of expenditures resulting from public projects to the group objective is markedly different from that afforded by the activities displaced by public investment.

fortunately, the difficulties of measurement alluded to in connection with the aggregate consumption objective are even more likely to be present in connection with the merit-want objective, since the external economies relevant to this objective are likely to be especially difficult to quantify. The cautionary words about expecting benefit-cost analysis to reflect all the pros and cons of a proposed investment bear emphasis.

The self-sufficiency objective. Of the categories of secondary benefits already mentioned, the principal ones relevant to the self-sufficiency objective are external economies and induced investment, and for these classes of benefits the remarks apropos of the aggregate consumption objective suffice. However, another category of secondary benefits, or secondary "dis-benefits" to be more precise, is relevant to the goal of self-sufficiency. Additions to aggregate consumption from public enterprise increase the demand for imports. Insofar as the level of imports responds—and licensing policy to the contrary notwithstanding, the level of consumer imports is undoubtedly to some extent sensitive to demand—these increases in demand must be counted as a liability on the self-sufficiency ledger of public investment programmes. If i denotes the marginal ratio of the value of imported consumer goods to total consumption, then

$$-i \times B_t$$

represents the indirect effect on self-sufficiency in year t of a public investment programme that contributes B_t to aggregate consumption. The indirect effect on self-sufficiency during the construction of a project will be positive if the expansion of public capital represented by the project is partly at the expense of private consumption. Symbolically the contribution is measured by the product

$$i(1 - \theta)K,$$

where $(1 - \theta)$ is the change in consumption accompanying a rupee change in investment (assuming that public investment does not mobilize otherwise unemployed resources) and K is the capital cost of the project.[1]

[1] See Chenery [*4*], pp. 87–93, for a further discussion as well as numerical estimates of the indirect effects of investment programmes on self-sufficiency.

Private Alternatives and Alternative Costs

The problem of private alternatives to public investment has already been faced in the discussion of intertemporal criteria. But alternatives enter the analysis of public investment not only as competitors for resources but also as competitors in fulfilling the demands that public sector projects are designed to meet. In general this competition presents no problem; indeed the existence of alternatives simplifies the measurement of willingness to pay by placing an upper bound on the amount that individuals are willing to spend for publicly produced goods and services. Problems arise only when specific private alternatives are mutually exclusive with public undertakings because construction of projects in the public sector would preempt the market, and the alternative source of supply in the private sector would therefore not come into existence.[1]

An example will illustrate the problem. Suppose economic analysis of a proposed addition to the capacity of railways indicates a capital cost of Re 1·0 per annual ton-mile and a perpetual aggregate consumption benefit (willingness to pay less operating costs) of 20 paise[2] per annual ton-mile. Now suppose that in the absence of the addition to railroad capacity, and only in its absence, private enterprise will undertake an addition to road transport capacity to serve roughly the same transport demands, and suppose that the capital cost of the private alternative is only 50 paise per annual ton-mile. In such circumstances, even though the aggregate consumption benefits per annual ton-mile might be somewhat less, and the contribution of the private alternative to objectives other than aggregate consumption substantially less, than the proposed railway addition, it might be desirable to abandon the public sector project in favour of the private alternative. This conclusion is even more likely in the event that a budgetary constraint leads

[1] A private alternative is also a special problem when technologically mutually exclusive with a public undertaking, as when the two must occupy the same site. The method for handling technological alternatives is to value the specific resources for which public and private investment compete in terms of the present value of the potential stream of benefits of the private alternative at the social rate of discount. This is simply an application of the criterion developed in the "Time and Interest" section earlier in this chapter.

[2] 100 paise = Re 1.

to an opportunity cost of public sector capital substantially in excess of the social price of private capital outlays.

It has been proposed that specific private alternatives for meeting the same demand as public projects be taken into account by limiting willingness to pay as a measure of benefits by the cost of the alternative.[1] In situations where the contribution of a private alternative not only to aggregate consumption but also to other objectives is the same as the contribution of a proposed public investment, to limit aggregate consumption benefits by alternative costs (provided alternative costs are measured on the same basis as the costs of public investment)[2] is to do no more than ensure fulfilment of the elementary requirement that, results being equal, the least-cost method of achieving the results is to be preferred over more costly methods. In general, however, when the contributions of the proposed public investment and the private alternative to the range of public policy goals differ, this simple device for taking private alternatives into account is inadequate. Even with just the aggregate consumption objective at issue, the contribution of the public and private alternatives may differ. The railroad addition mentioned in the previous paragraph will move some goods more cheaply, motor transport other goods, and these differences will in general be reflected in differences in the composition of railroad and truck shipments. Hence the aggregate consumption cost of the truck alternative is not an adequate surrogate for the aggregate consumption benefits of railroad.

A more general procedure is the following: Consider specific private alternatives to different packages of public investment as a set of responses to public decisions and add their benefits and costs to the benefits and costs of the associated public investment (public and private benefits and costs being calculated on the same basis). In this approach, the maximal private alternative generally becomes the private response to a "zero" public

[1] See, among others, the *Green Book* [*28*], p. 42, and *Budget Circular A-47* [*27*], p. 8, both of which suggest the use of alternative (steam) costs as an upper bound to the benefits of any proposed development of hydroelectric energy.

[2] Thus taxes are not to be considered an element of private cost; shadow wage rates and factor prices must replace money wages and prices when real and money values differ; and so forth.

investment package, this is, to no public project at all. The private road transport industry, for example, might be expected to expand its capacity most in the absence of any expansion in rail service,[1] with progressively smaller expansion in response to successively larger increments in the capacity of the railroads.

The drawback of this approach[2] is the extra data about private intentions, costs, and benefits that must be gathered and processed for the economic analysis of public sector projects. At present I see no satisfactory alternative; complexity of analysis is the price of systematic decision-making.

Pricing Policy for Public Enterprise

Pricing policy, as an aspect of the operation of projects rather than of their design, might be considered outside the scope of the present discussion. However, the intimate relationship between the operation of projects and the fulfilment of the goals that prompt the original sacrifice necessary to bring them into being makes at least cursory attention to pricing policy a necessary part of the formulation of criteria for public investment.

On the other hand, the relationship between pricing policy and design decisions can be over-emphasized. Although the financial feasibility of a proposed investment must inevitably be a chief, if not the only, consideration in the private sector of mixed-enterprise economies, one advantage of public enterprise is that narrow profit and loss considerations need not dominate investment decisions. Thus the possibility of recovering costs (through revenues) should not necessarily be decisive in the allocation of public investment funds, nor should cost recovery determine pricing policy for public projects once they are in existence. Even when aggregate consumption benefits exceed aggregate consumption costs—and in view of the other objectives of public policy they need not to justify a public undertaking—it may be infeasible to recover costs. A large portion of aggregate consumption benefits may in certain instances take

[1] This will not be as likely, however, in the presence of complementarity between rail and road transport.

[2] Its details are spelled out in Maass and others [*16*], pp. 206–219.

the form of external economies or of "public" goods (like flood control) for which it is practically impossible to levy charges equal to the benefits received.[1] In addition it may be impossible to recapture more than a small fraction of the consumers' surplus enjoyed on vendible goods and services like electric energy and public transportation, even though multiple tariffs and similar devices permit public authorities to transfer more of the gains afforded by public sector projects from the direct beneficiaries to the community as a whole than do uniform prices.

And even when it is possible to recapture benefits by means of high prices for the goods and services produced in the public sector, to do so may conflict with other objectives of public policy. It was shown earlier in this volume that pricing policy is a direct determinant of benefits with respect to redistributional objectives, and pricing policy can indirectly affect the fulfilment of other objectives as well.

The prices charged for publicly produced goods and services have a direct bearing on the aggregate consumption that results from their provision. Pricing in accordance with "what the traffic will bear" may be considered a cruel and unusual punishment by users of project outputs, but it well may be the most effective way of ensuring that publicly produced goods and services end up in the uses for which their value is highest. In any event the converse seems to be indisputable: If prices fail altogether to reflect demands, it will be impossible to employ direct rationing and other devices to realize the full aggregate consumption potential of public sector projects.

Against this argument for relatively high prices to aid in rationing project outputs in accordance with their most productive uses must be placed an argument for low prices to ensure the quick response of potential users to the existence of public projects. It may be necessary to convince potential users that there are profits to be earned from employing public sector outputs in their economic activities, and concessional prices may be the most effective means of convincing sceptics. Such a situation might occur in the extension of irrigation to previously

[1] On the problem posed by public goods, illuminating articles are Paul Samuelson [*24*], [*25*], [*26*]. See also Richard Musgrave [*22*], pp. 42–89, and Maass and others [*16*], pp. 44–47.

dry-farming areas. A word of caution, however, is in order with respect to promotional pricing: Although the case for price concessions in the early years of a project's life may be sound, arguments (other than redistribution) for perpetuating concessional pricing beyond, say, five to ten years seem less compelling. Yet in the interest of equity, price increases as the project matures should not come as a surprise to project users.

As I have tried to emphasize throughout this discussion, maximization of aggregate consumption is by no means the only objective of public policy. Promotion of self-sufficiency and merit-want objectives, as well as of the redistribution objective, may dictate departures from the pricing policy that would contribute most to the aggregate consumption objective.

And even though redistribution may not be an explicit goal of a particular public investment, distributional considerations inevitably enter into pricing decisions, for price determines the division of the gains of the public investment between the project users and the community as a whole. The higher the revenues are, the lower the general taxation required to supply a given level of public services and public investment, and the lower the effective demand in the hands of project users. Hence the private consumption of the community as a whole, project users apart, can be higher without impairing the provision of public services or investment.

Reinvestment is another factor in setting price policy. It has been shown that when the marginal internal rate of return and the marginal social rate of discount differ, the rate at which benefits are reinvested bears on the effectiveness of public investment. And the reinvestment rate can very likely be increased by high prices that transfer command over future resources from the private sector into public hands; the difference between social and private rates of discount means that, relative to private allocation of resources, the public sector will allocate a large proportion of the output of capital goods to increasing the capacity of capital-goods producing industries and a smaller proportion to increasing the capacity of consumer-goods industries. Indeed the logic of reinvestment—were this the only consideration—would lead to a pricing policy resembling that of a discriminatory monopolist who captures all the consumers' surplus he can.[1]

The last of the considerations entering into pricing decisions has already been briefly alluded to in the discussion of promotional pricing: the conflict between the desire for flexibility in prices as a means of responding to changing conditions and the desire for certainty about future prices on the part of project users in order to justify the investment required to make effective use of project outputs. The conflict can in part be resolved, as has already been suggested with regard to promotional pricing, by announcing the duration of price concessions in advance. But where changes in conditions cannot be foreseen, the conflict becomes more acute. To some extent it can be resolved by contracts or by guarantees of price ceilings on public outputs for a sufficient number of years to justify the private investment deemed desirable by public authorities. However, the public interest should be protected by escape clauses permitting changes in the prices or distribution of public outputs, upon payment of indemnities, to reflect unexpected changes in demand that make alternative uses more attractive from the viewpoint of public policy than the uses originally contemplated.

To summarize, the principal considerations in the formulation of pricing policies for public enterprise are (1) the fulfilment of the multiple goals of public policy discussed in Chapter 1, (2) the distribution of gains from public enterprise between project users and the nation at large, (3) the reinvestment of benefits, and (4) the conflict between flexibility and certainty. The relative importance attached to each of these considerations must inevitably be a value judgment.

The total effect of this discussion of pricing policies may appear to be negative, and indeed it has been largely designed to demonstrate the complexity of pricing decisions for a government that is pursuing a multiplicity of goals in its development policy. The futility of basing pricing policy on such simple rules

[1] An alternative to a pricing policy designed to maximize public command over resources is one designed to place outputs in the hands of private economic units that will reinvest rather than consume the benefits they earn even though such a policy may lead to a reduction in the value of public sector outputs as measured by willingness to pay.

as "price equal to marginal cost" emerges as a corollary. And if the dictates of efficiency-oriented welfare economics are insufficient guide rules, how much more wanting are private sector rates of return and depreciation policies. Indeed I should hope it superfluous to add at this point that private sector rates of return and depreciation policies are totally irrelevant to the formulation of public sector pricing policies. This is not to deny that reference to private sector practices may be useful in the propaganda war that may be required to implement public sector pricing policies determined in accordance with the considerations just discussed. But the propaganda tail should not wag the policy dog.

CHAPTER 3

A SELECTIVE SUMMARY

The point of departure for this essay has been that for benefit-cost analysis to serve an effective and useful role in the implementation of planned economic development, the multiplicity of goals of public policy must be explicitly reflected in the standards and criteria that govern public investment. It is of secondary importance and purely a matter of planning convenience whether the multiplicity of goals is reflected in the form of explicit weights on the contribution of public sector programmes to specific objectives of public policy or in the form of constraints on programme performance with respect to different goals. What matters is that no relevant objective of public policy is ignored or subordinated in an ordering that brings it to bear only if "other things are equal"—which in the nature of the universe "other things" never are.

Because objectives are not fully complementary, policymakers must make value judgments about their relative importance; these value judgments are reflected in public investment criteria in the shadow prices that replace market prices in calculating benefits and costs. Project plan formulation ideally takes place in three stages: first, the national economic plan setting the broad strategy of development is elaborated; second, shadow prices—weights on objectives, rates of discount, and others—are derived from comparisons of the national plan with rejected alternatives; third, projects are designed to carry out the strategic decisions of the plan. It is in the first stage that policymakers' value judgments enter: by choosing one national economic plan over alternatives and designating it as the optimal plan. Consider, for example, how the choice between alternative national economic plans affects the social rate of discount for the aggregate consumption objective. Alternatives *A* and *B* both might provide an increase in consumption of 50% ten years from now, but alternative *A* might provide for an annual growth rate of 4% beyond the ten-year horizon and require investment every year equal to 12% of gross national product, while alternative *B* provides post-terminal growth in consumption of 6% per year and requires investment equal to 20% of gross national product to achieve the higher target. The choice between the two plans requires a value judgment between more cake today and tomorrow (*A*) and more cake the day after tomorrow (*B*); of the two plans *A* implies a higher consumption rate of discount.

It is clear that if policymakers are to lead, they must be presented by planners with a range of alternative national plans from which to choose. By elaborating only one national economic plan, technicians effectively arrogate to themselves policymaking functions which ought to be performed by those whom the body politic has selected for the role of leadership.[1] Division of labour between technicians and policymakers is quite consistent with feedback between the two. Initially plans must be framed on the basis of highly aggregated and imperfect knowledge. Consequently, neither the targets explicit nor the shadow prices implicit in a national economic plan are inviolable. On the contrary, the implementation of the plan—the process of project formulation and selection—will suggest revision both of plan targets and shadow prices. Suppose the national plan calls for an increase of Rs 100 crores in Transylvanistan's annual consumption over ten years and implies at the same time a premium of 0·8 on Transylvan consumption relative to aggregate consumption. If the ensemble of projects formulated on the basis of the weight of 0·8 appear

[1] It is an oversimplification to suggest that when a single plan is elaborated policymakers are denied any participation in planning. The plan inevitably reflects a variety of compromises among mutually conflicting goals. But reflecting these compromises in a single plan blurs the choices and the trade-offs among different objectives. It also makes it easier to incorporate the wishes of special interests into the plan; when choices are never clearly spelled out, it is impossible to distinguish the weight which the Government places on the income of Transylvanistan relative to the nation as a whole from the weight Transylvan interest groups place on their own incomes and are able by one means or another to incorporate into the national economic plan. Subjecting alternative plans to the harsh light of public criticism makes it harder for special interests to hold sway against the national interest when the two are at variance.

to promise Rs 125 crores to Transylvanistan, then either the original target must be increased, or the premium must be decreased and project plans modified.

No attempt will be made to summarize all the specific criteria proposed in this volume, for the discussion of most of the individual criteria has been a summary. But certain points perhaps bear emphasis. The notion that the meaning of benefits and costs varies from objective to objective is perhaps an obvious one, yet I know of no attempt to follow out the logical consequences of this point in benefit-cost analysis. One illustration of the functional dependence of benefits and costs on objectives lies in the contrast between the role of project revenues in measuring aggregate consumption benefits and their role in measuring redistributional benefits. With respect to aggregate consumption, benefits are measured by the amount project users are *willing* to pay for goods and services provided by the project, and actual revenues are simply transfer payments from users of project outputs to the nation as a whole. With respect to redistributional objectives, on the other hand, benefits are measured by the *difference* between what project users are willing to pay and what they actually pay, for this difference determines the consumption gains of project users. Similarly, the consumption created through the multiplier by the expenditure of project users is not counted as a benefit from the point of view of the aggregate consumption objective because it is assumed that a corresponding multiplier chain would result from investment anywhere else in the economy. From the point of view of redistribution to a particular region, however, the potential multiplier chain outside the region is of no moment.

The choice of an intertemporal criterion has received more attention in this study than any other problem. The procedure proposed for intertemporal comparisons among alternative investment programmes is to impose weights on the contributions to each objective in each time period. The weights may be explicit or, by means of constraints, implicit. If weights are chosen explicitly and the weight on present aggregate consumption is set equal to unity, the proposed criterion becomes simply the familiar present-value criterion. The question of choice of weights for various time periods then becomes a question of choice of a discount rate. The frequently heard proposal that the appropriate rate of discount for the public sector is the marginal internal rate of return in the private sector is questioned in this study on the grounds that, even leaving aside differences between private and public concepts of benefits and costs, the argument for the use of the private rate of return is based on a misapplication of Irving Fisher's contributions to capital theory [*8*]. Fisher was able to divorce the decisions of (1) choosing an investment programme and (2) distributing consumption over time according to one's intertemporal preferences by assuming that the investor can always borrow and lend unlimited amounts at a given market rate of interest. A Fisherian investor can choose the investment programme that has the highest present value at the market rate of interest and then redistribute the income from the programme over time by borrowing or lending in accordance with his subjective preferences. I contend that no analogous mechanism for redistributing consumption over time is open to the public sector in a mixed-enterprise economy and therefore that the government, unlike an individual in a perfect capital market, cannot abdicate to the judgment of the market the choice of the discount rate by which the present values of alternative programmes are computed. A value judgment about the intertemporal distribution of benefits must be incorporated into the investment criteria.

There are good reasons for supposing that the *social* discount rate that a community would choose in its collective, political capacity differs from the *private* discount rate that would emerge from the community's market decisions even if capital markets were perfectly competitive. This does not mean that the marginal rate of return in the private sector is totally irrelevant to public sector decisions, for if the marginal rate of return of benefits differs from the social rate of discount, the nominal price of public investment funds of Re 1 per rupee must be replaced by a shadow price that reflects the present value, at the social rate of discount, of private utilization of resources alternative to public investment. The higher the private sector returns are relative to the social rate of discount, the higher the shadow price on public capital outlays. The shadow price also depends on the extent of reinvestment of benefits. (The details of this dependence are spelled out in the discussion of intertemporal criteria.)

The shadow price of capital is not a discount rate (its dimensions differ from those of a discount rate) and should not be confused with one. It is possible, however, to combine the shadow price of capital and the social rate of discount into a set of "synthetic" rates of discount for use with the nominal price of capital of Re 1 per rupee. If the shadow price of capital exceeds unity, the synthetic rate of discount decreases with the longevity of projects, as Table 2.1 illustrates; in other words, if public sector investments of different longevities are to be equally effective at the margin and if the shadow price of capital exceeds unity, the shorter the life of a project, the higher must be its marginal internal rate of return.

The "social-rate-of-discount-cum-opportunity-cost" criterion outlined in Chapter 2 and the conventional criterion of evaluating present values at the private sector rate of return share a common purpose of ensuring that public investment is as effective at the margin as the alternative private use of resources. The intertemporal criterion proposed here, however, unlike its more conventional rival, does not unduly discriminate against durable projects (like water-resources development). This is perhaps most clearly shown in the synthetic discount rate form of the criterion, in which the cutoff rate of return declines progressively with durability.

It should be noted that although the present value criterion is the recommended basis for intertemporal comparisons, naïve use of this criterion can lead to gross errors in the timing of the construction of projects when benefit rates increase over time. The section on "Dynamics" in Chapter 2 illustrates the problem and proposes a simple corrective device.

The contribution of this essay to the problems of risk and uncertainty consists mostly in pointing out that aversion to uncertainty, which takes the form of conservative estimates of benefits and costs, additions of risk premiums to discount rates, and conservative estimates of the economic lives of projects, is not necessarily the appropriate attitude for a government, especially in the analysis of independent projects in relation to aggregative objectives. The fact that the failure or below par performance of some projects may be balanced by an unexpected degree of success of others allows a government to concentrate more on expected values, and to worry less about the dispersion of outcomes, of individual projects than private investors can afford to do.

The term "secondary benefits" is used here as a catch-all to describe the indirect contributions that projects make to the various objectives of public policy, that is, contributions other than those reflected in the direct utilization of project outputs. For the aggregate consumption objective, secondary benefits arise one way or another from violations of the competitive model that the world perversely perpetrates. For other objectives, however, the contributions of projects through secondary benefits are more far-reaching and may often be of greater significance than their direct contributions. The contributions of projects to a regional redistribution objective through the multiplier chain of expenditures, to which allusion has already been made in this summary, illustrate this point.

The existence of private alternatives for meeting the demands that occasion public investment presents special problems in benefit-cost analysis when the private and public measures are mutually exclusive. I have attempted to point out the defects inherent in limiting willingness to pay as a measure of aggregate consumption benefits by the cost of the private alternative. A more general procedure has been sketched out in this study, and reference made to a more detailed exposition.

This discussion of specific criteria concludes with a brief discussion of the principles of pricing decisions for public enterprise. Although private sector rates of return have a limited role in the intertemporal criterion for the design of public investment programmes, the rates of return and depreciation policies of the private sector are totally irrelevant to public sector pricing decisions. Rather, the relevant considerations in the formulation of pricing policies for public enterprise are (1) the fulfilment of the multiple goals of public policy which are discussed in Chapter 1, (2) the distribution of gains from public enterprise between project users and the nation at large, (3) the reinvestment of benefits, and (4) the conflict between the need for flexibility and the need for certainty.

My purpose has not been to write a handbook of criteria for

benefit-cost analysis of public sector projects but to combine the relevant parts of the theory of economic decision-making (the theory of the firm or the household) and the theory of welfare economics in order to provide a basis on which a handbook of criteria might be written. Largely this has meant devising ways and means to take into account the additional complexity of the utility function of a government as against the utility function of a firm or a household. Whether or not the ways and means proposed here represent an acceptable foundation for public investment criteria, I, as a partisan, am not in a position to judge. In any event the handbook of criteria that is the goal of this exercise cannot be written without much more attention to the problems of administrative feasibility than has entered into this discussion, for a balance must be struck between theoretical rigour and limitations of data and personnel.

REFERENCES

1 Armen A. Alchian. "The Rate of Interest, Fisher's Rate of Return over Costs and Keynes' Internal Rate of Return," *American Economic Review*, Vol. XLV, No. 5 (December 1955), pp. 938–943.

2 Kenneth Arrow. "Optimal Capital Policy, the Cost of Capital, and Myopic Decision Rules," *Annals of the Institute of Statistical Mathematics*, Vol. XVI (1964), Nos. 1–2, pp. 21–30.

3 Jagdish Bhagwati. "The Pure Theory of International Trade: A Survey," *The Economic Journal*, Vol. LXXIV, No. 293 (March 1964), pp. 1–84.

4 Hollis Chenery. "The Application of Investment Criteria," *Quarterly Journal of Economics*, Vol. LXVII, No. 1 (February 1953), pp. 76–96.

5 Maurice Dobb. *Economic Theory and Socialism*. New York: International Publishers, 1955.

6 Maurice Dobb. *Political Theory and Capitalism*. New York: International Publishers, 1945.

7 Jules Dupuit. "On the Measurement of the Utility of Public Works," first published in *Annales des Ponts et Chaussées*, Sér. 2, No. 8 (1844); English translation in *International Economic Papers*, No. 2. London: Macmillan, 1952.

8 Irving Fisher. *The Theory of Interest: As Determined by Impatience to Spend Income and Opportunity to Invest It*, originally published in 1930; republished New York: Augustus M. Kelly, 1961.

9 Christopher Foster. *The Transport Problem*. London: Blackie, 1963.

10 Milton Friedman. *Essays in Positive Economics*. Chicago: University of Chicago Press, 1953.

11 John R. Hicks. *Value and Capital*. 2nd ed. London: Oxford University Press, 1946.

12 Government of India. Planning Commission, Perspective Planning Division. *Perspectives of Development, 1961–1976: Implications of Planning for a Minimum Level of Living*. New Delhi, 1962. Mimeographed.

13 Indian Statistical Institute. *Economic Strategy and the Third Plan*. Bombay: Asia Publishing House, 1963.

14 International Labour Office. *Employment Objectives in Economic Development: Report of a Meeting of Experts*. Geneva, 1961.

15 Oskar Lange, ed. *Problems of Political Economy of Socialism*. New Delhi: People's Publishing House, 1962.

16 Arthur Maass, Maynard Hufschmidt, Robert Dorfman, Harold A. Thomas, Jr., Stephen A. Marglin, and Gordon M. Fair. *Design of Water-Resource Systems: New Techniques for Relating Economic Objectives, Engineering Analysis, and Governmental Planning*. Cambridge, Mass.: Harvard University Press, 1962.

17 Alan S. Manne. "Capacity Expansion and Probabalistic Growth," *Econometrica*, Vol. 29, No. 4 (October 1961), pp. 632–649.

18 Stephen A. Marglin. *Approaches to Dynamic Investment Planning*. Amsterdam: North Holland, 1963.

19 Stephen A. Marglin. "The Opportunity Costs of Public Investment," *Quarterly Journal of Economics*, Vol. LXXVII, No. 2 (May 1963), pp. 274–289.
20 Stephen A. Marglin. "The Social Rate of Discount and the Optimal Rate of Investment," *Quarterly Journal of Economics*, Vol. LXXVII, No. 1 (February 1963), pp. 95–111.
21 Pierre Massé. *Optimal Investment Decisions: Rules for Action and Criteria for Choice*. Englewood Cliffs, N.J.: Prentice-Hall, 1962.
22 Richard Musgrave. *The Theory of Public Finance: A Study in Public Economy*. New York: McGraw-Hill, 1959.
23 Paul N. Rosenstein-Rodan, ed. *Pricing and Fiscal Policies: A Study in Method*. London: Allen and Unwin; Cambridge, Mass.: The M.I.T. Press, 1964.
24 Paul Samuelson. "Aspects of Public Expenditure Theories," *The Review of Economics and Statistics*, Vol. XL, No. 4 (November 1958), pp. 332–338.
25 Paul Samuelson. "Diagrammatic Exposition of a Theory of Public Expenditure," *The Review of Economics and Statistics*, Vol. XXXVII, No. 4 (November 1955), pp. 350–356.
26 Paul Samuelson. "The Pure Theory of Public Expenditure," *The Review of Economics and Statistics*, Vol. XXXVI, No. 4 (November 1954), pp. 387–389.
27 United States Government. Bureau of the Budget. *Budget Circular A-47*. Washington, 1952. Hectograph.
28 United States Government. Federal Inter-Agency River Basin Committee, Subcommittee on Benefits and Costs. *Proposed Practices for Economic Analyses of River Basin Projects* (*Green Book*). Washington, May 1950; revised, May 1958.
29 United States Government. Panel of Consultants to the Bureau of the Budget (Maynard M. Hufschmidt, Chairman, John Krutilla, Julius Margolis, with Stephen A. Marglin as assistant). *Standards and Criteria for Formulating and Evaluating Federal Water Resources Development*. (*Consultants' Report*.) Washington, 1961. Mimeographed.
30 United States Government. *Policies, Standards, and Procedures in the Formulation, Evaluation, and Review of Plans for Use and Development of Water and Related Land Resources*. Senate Document No. 97, 87th Congress. Washington, 1962.

INDEX

For Product Safety Concerns and Information please contact our EU representative GPSR@taylorandfrancis.com
Taylor & Francis Verlag GmbH, Kaufingerstraße 24, 80331 München, Germany

www.ingramcontent.com/pod-product-compliance
Ingram Content Group UK Ltd.
Pitfield, Milton Keynes, MK11 3LW, UK
UKHW021501240926
475702UK00035B/87

* 9 7 8 1 1 3 8 8 3 0 6 5 3 *